This Book belongs to:

....

ALPHABET

CONNECT THE DOTS

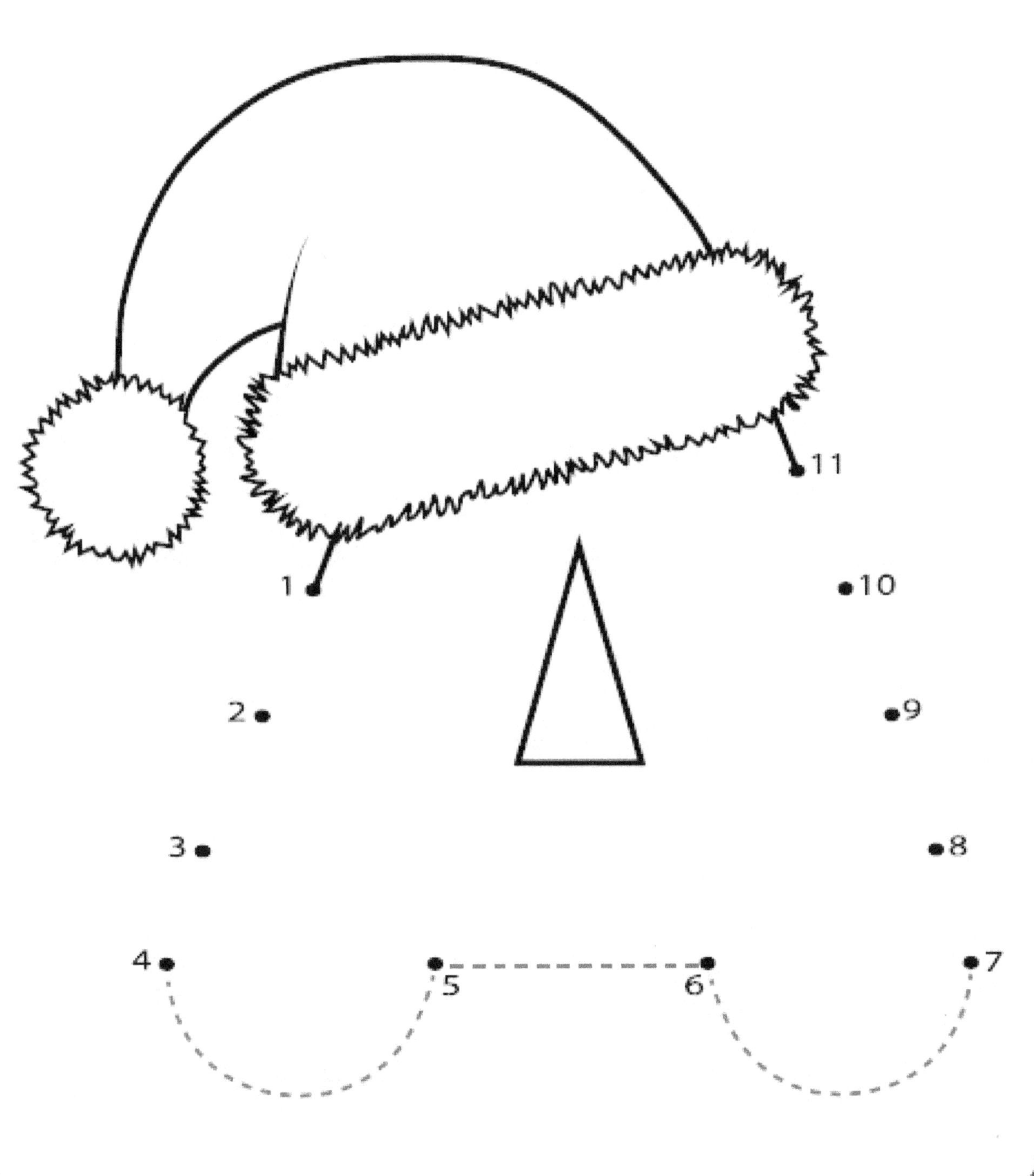

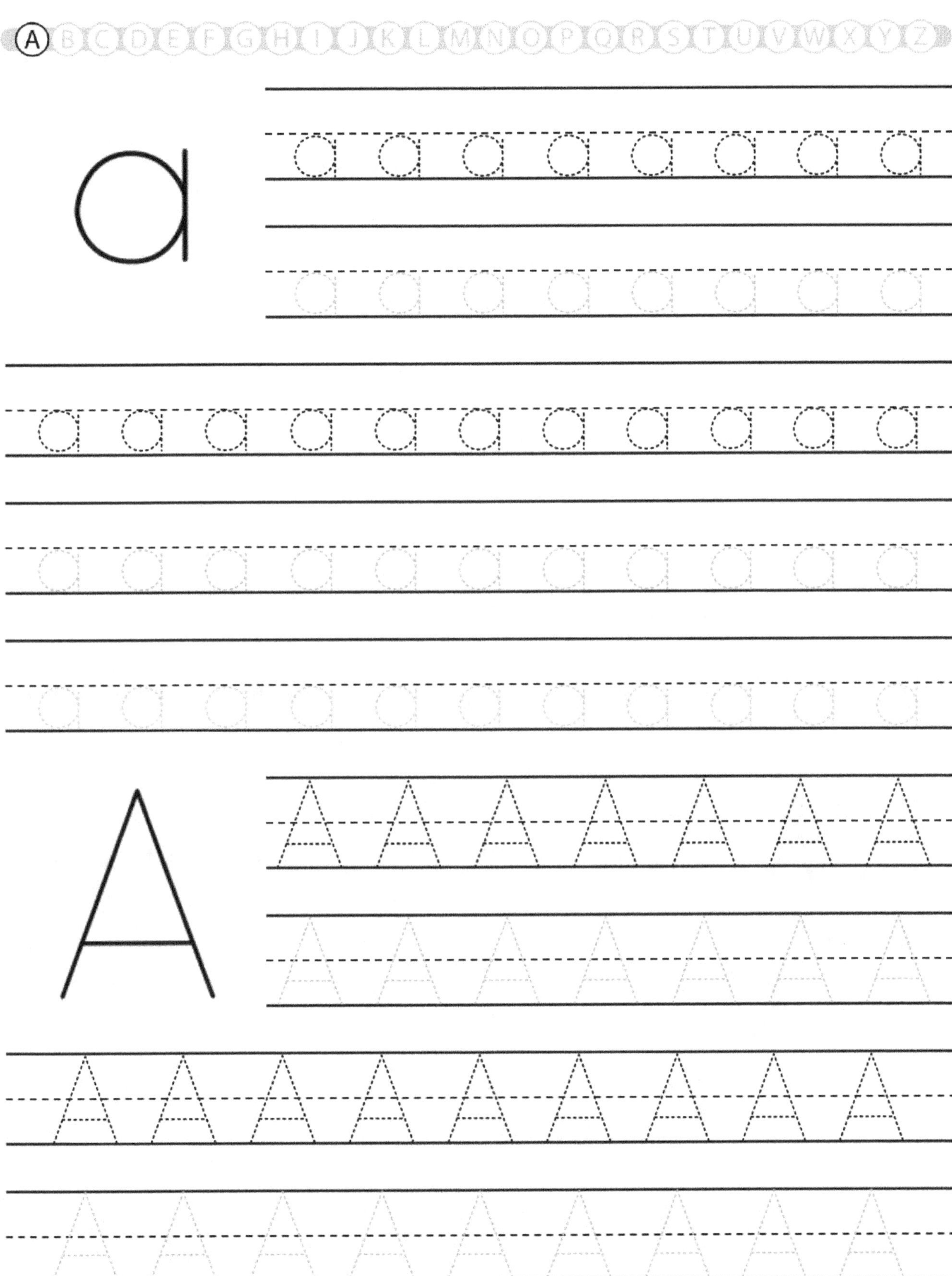

CONNECT THE DOTS

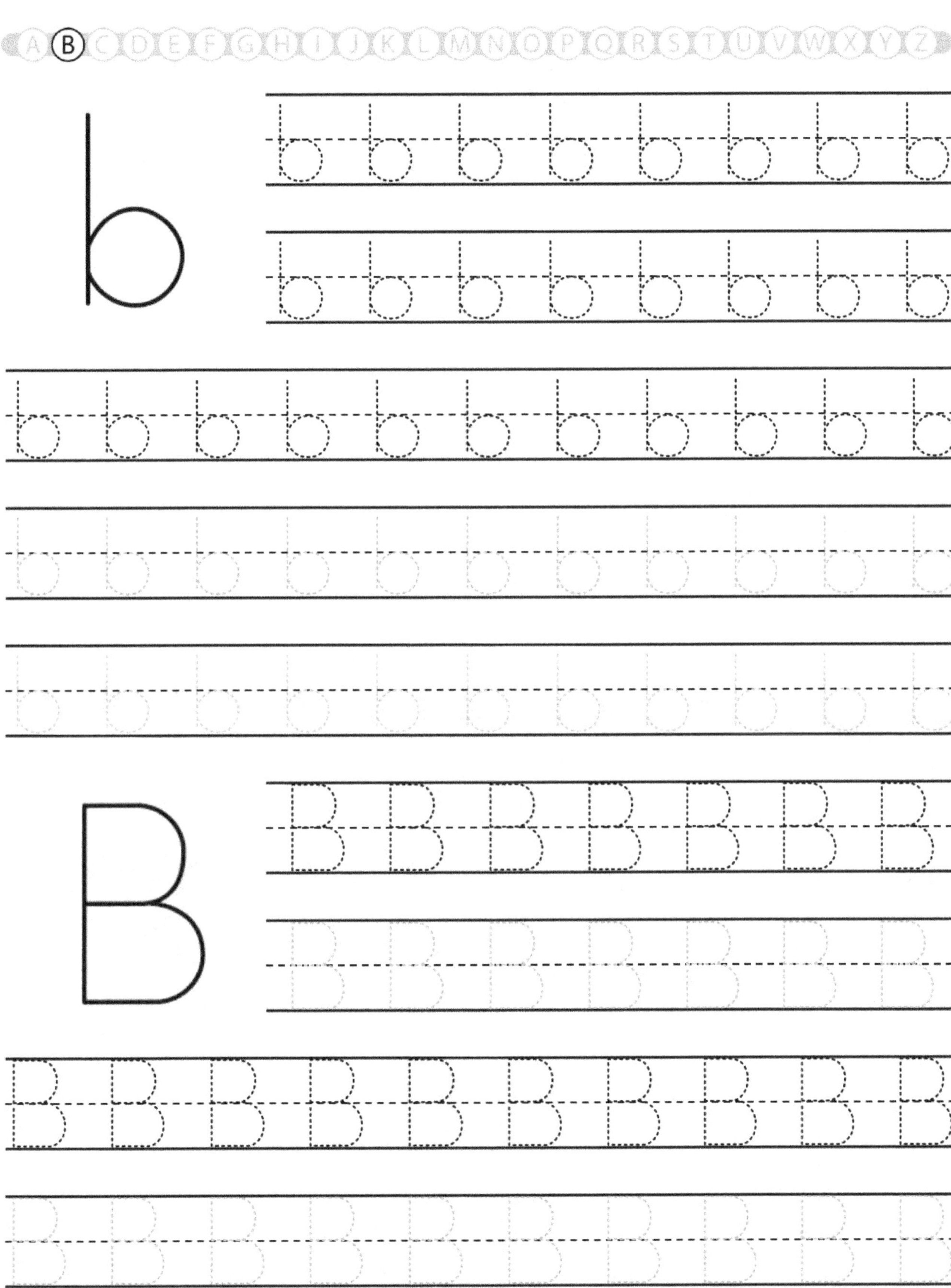

CONNECT THE DOTS

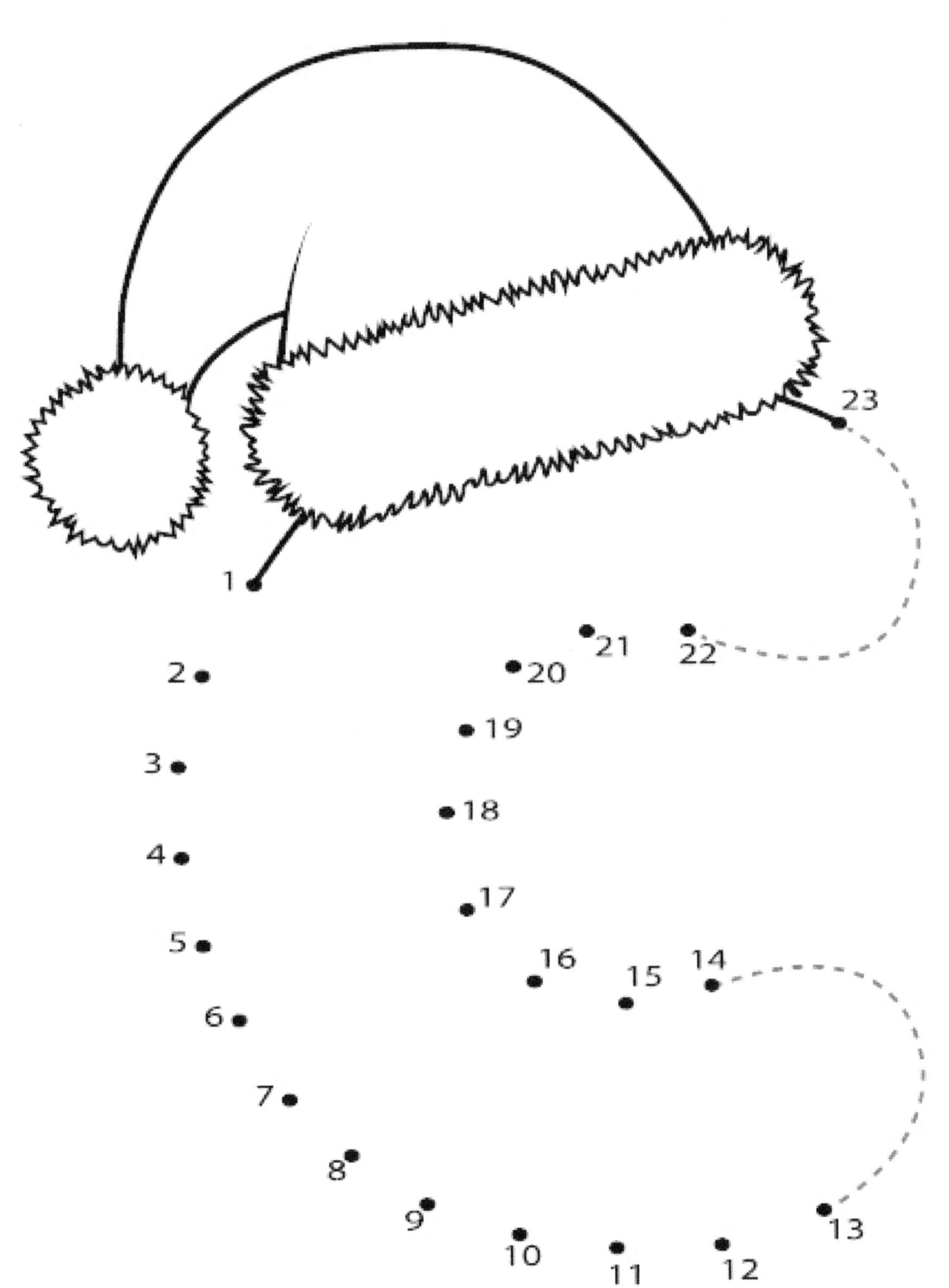

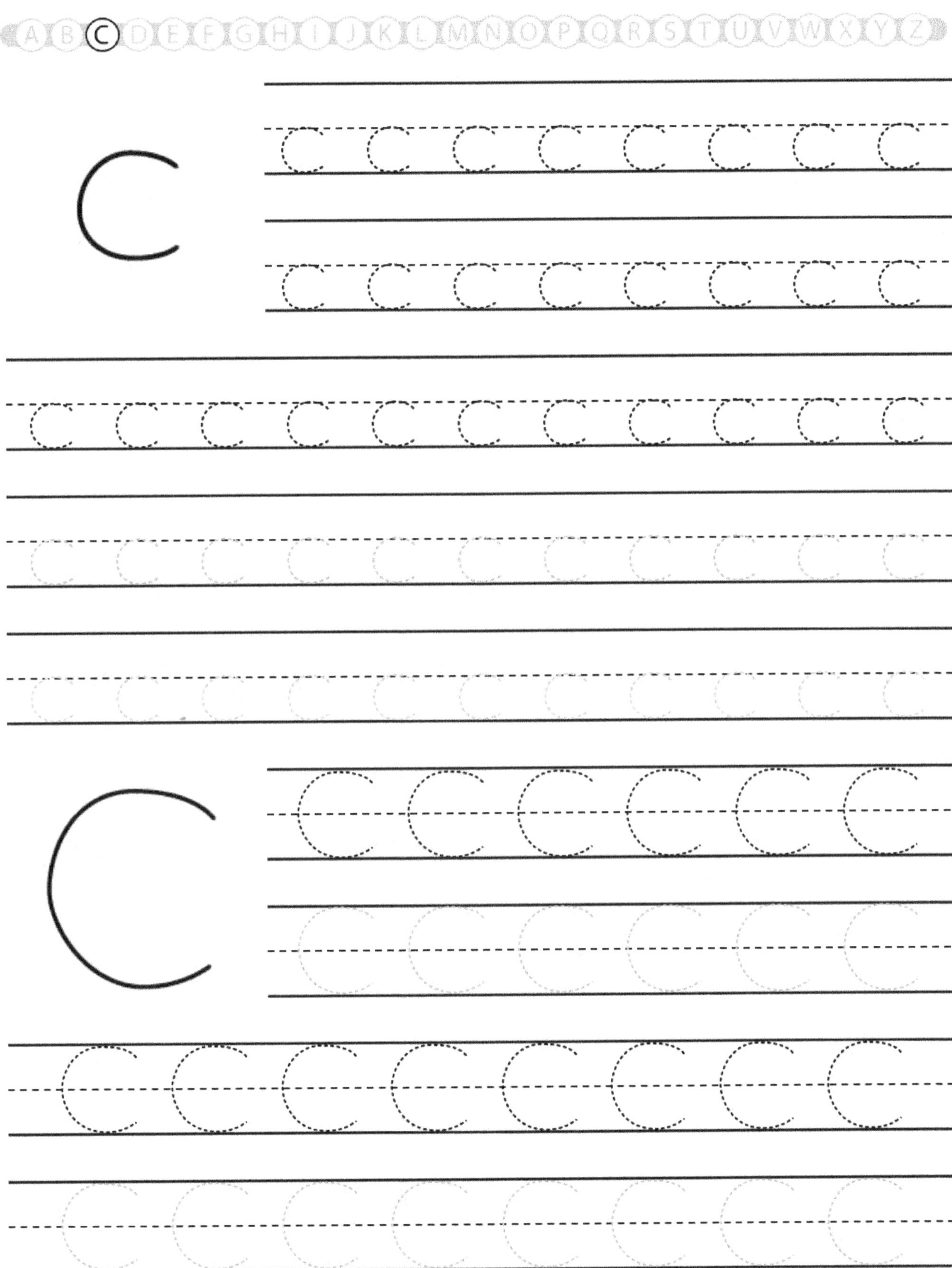

CONNECT THE DOTS

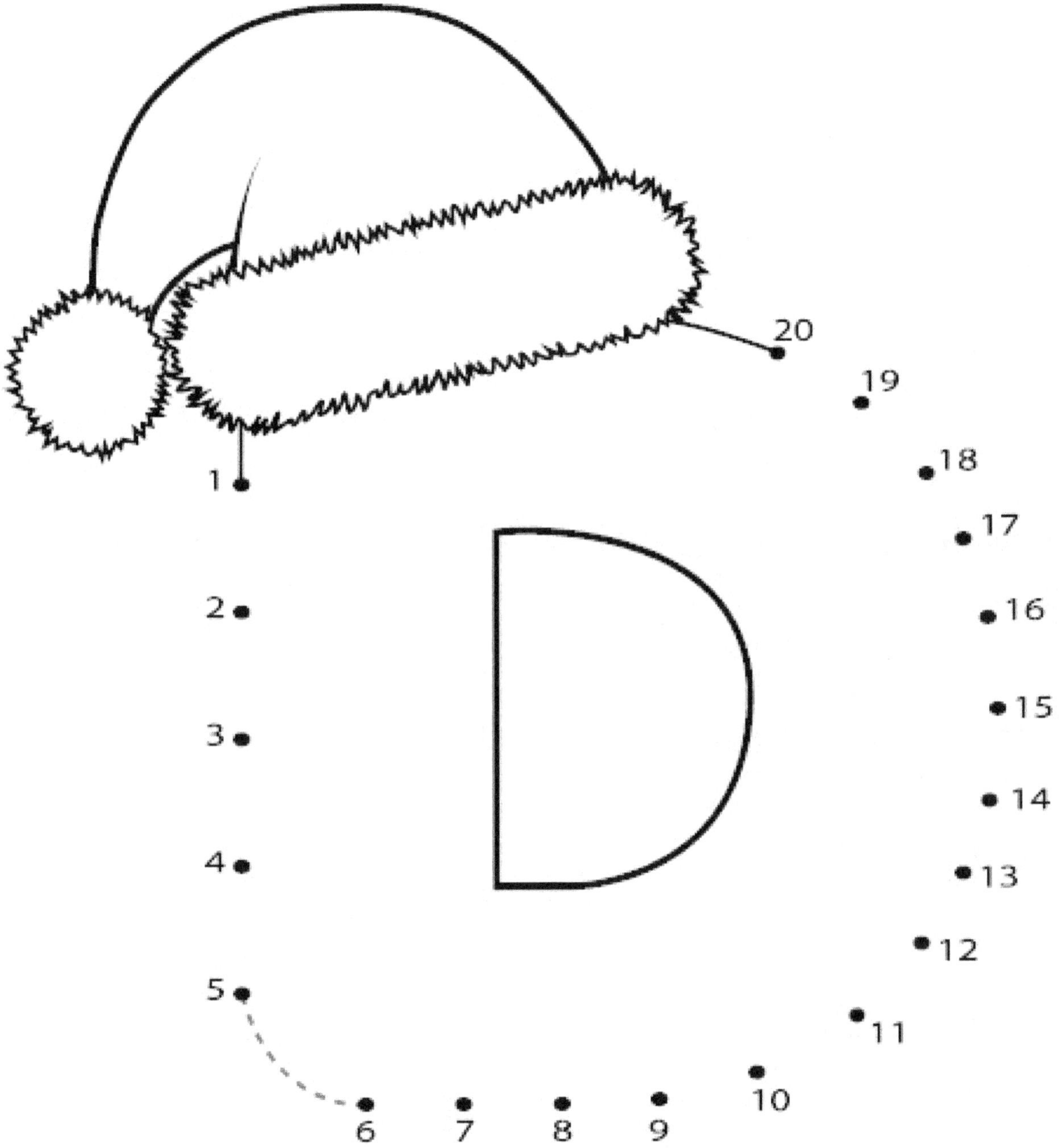

20

19

18

17

1

16

2

15

3

14

4

13

12

5

11

6   7   8   9   10

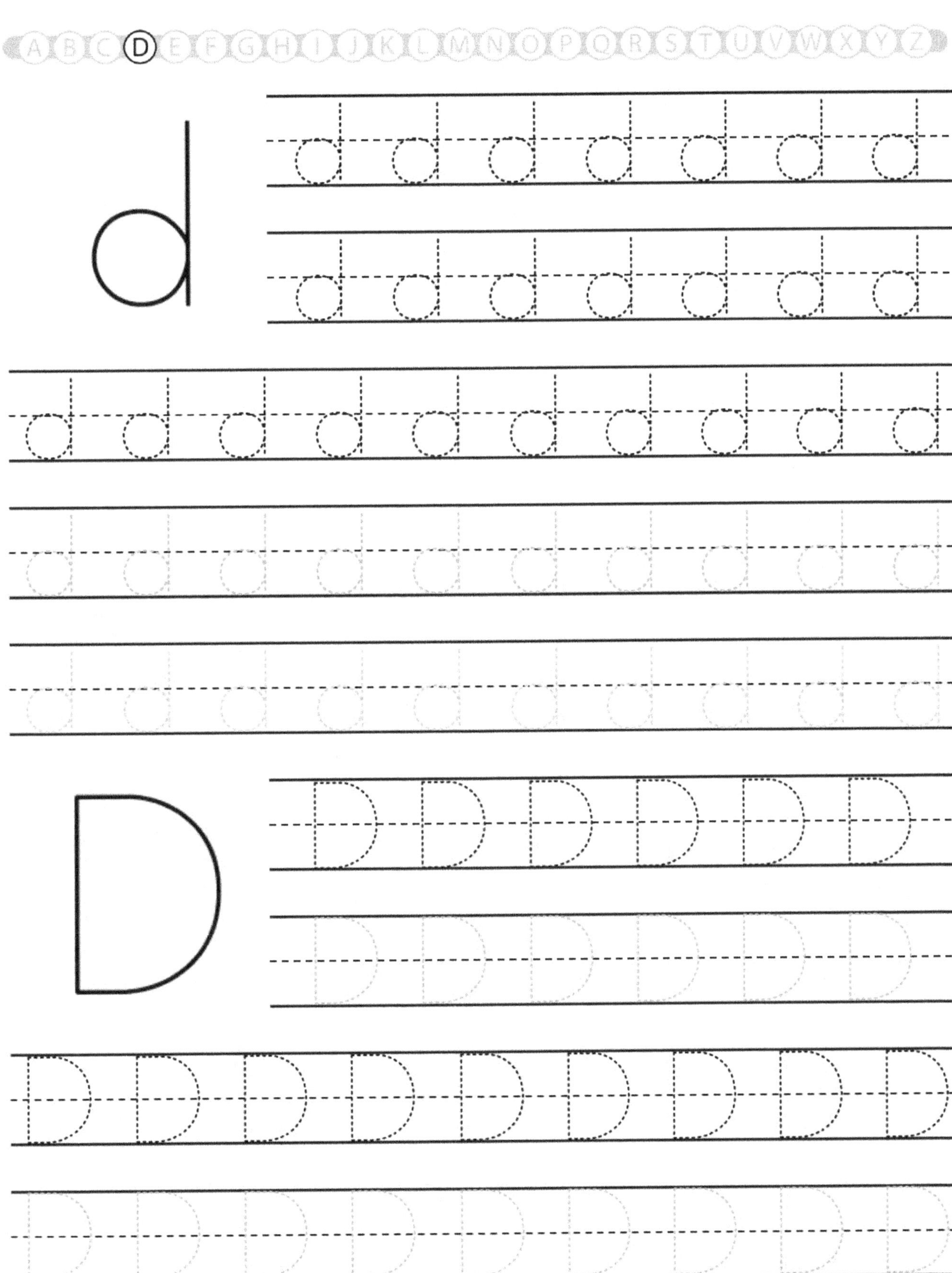

CONNECT THE DOTS

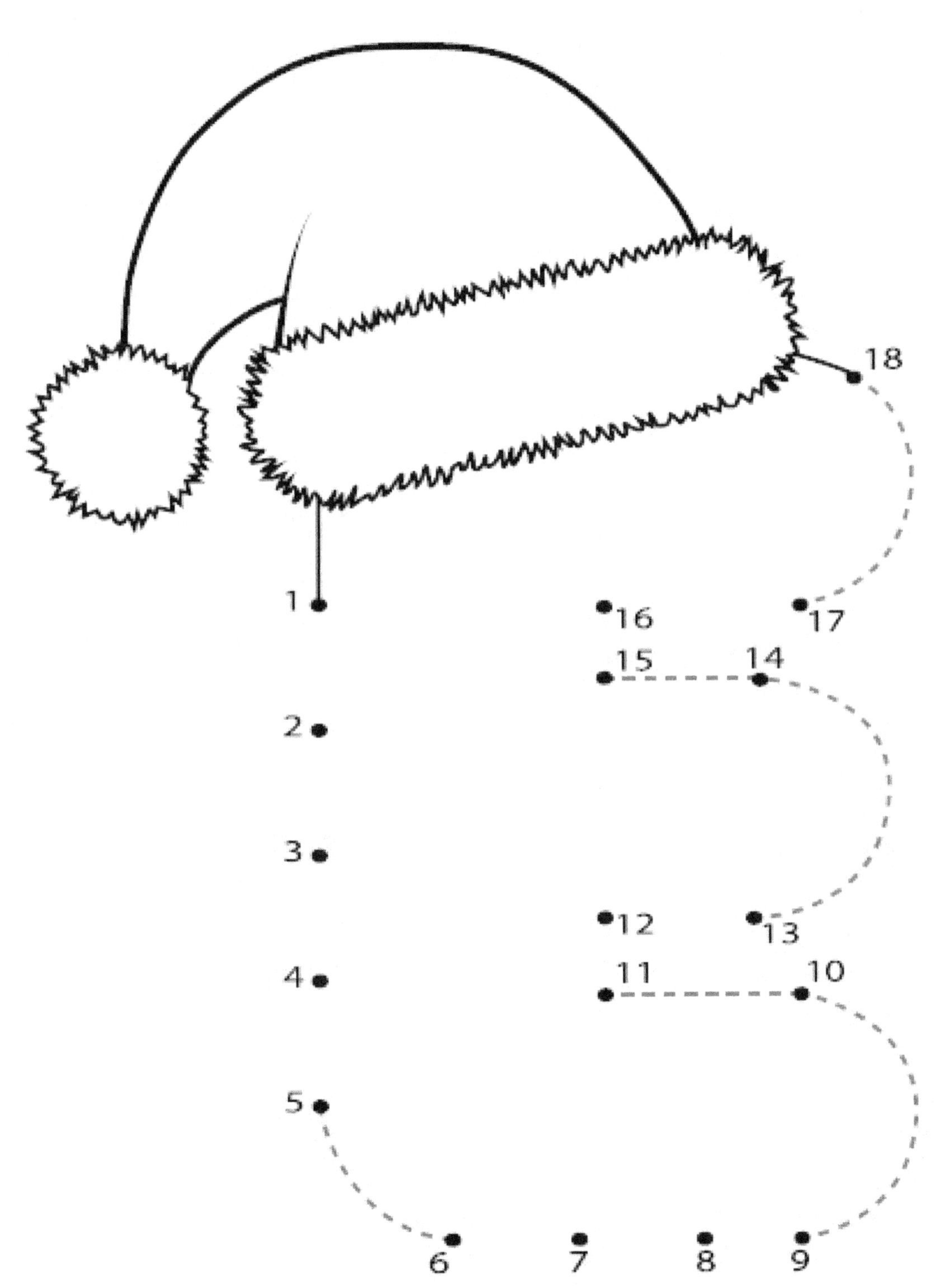

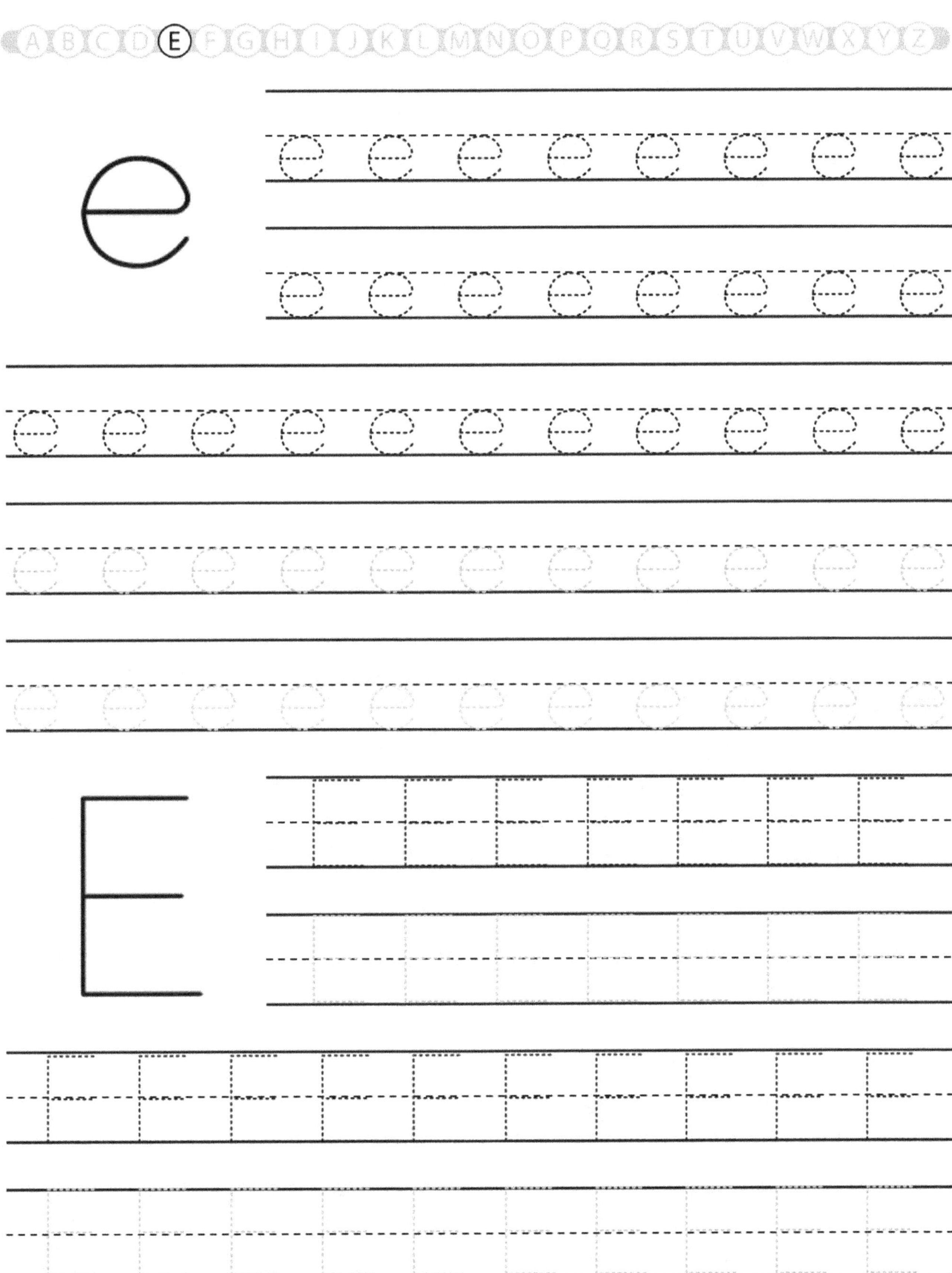

CONNECT THE DOTS

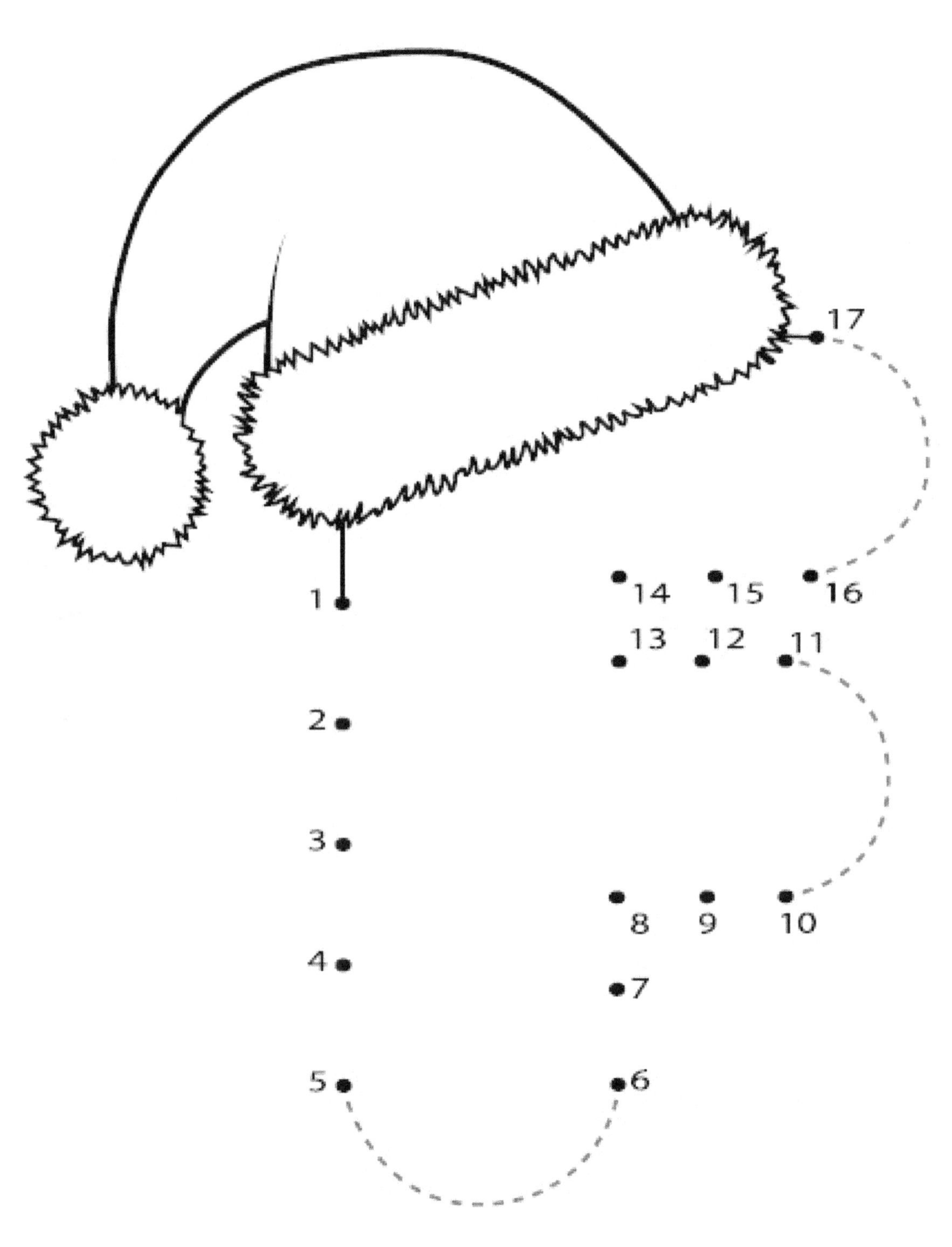

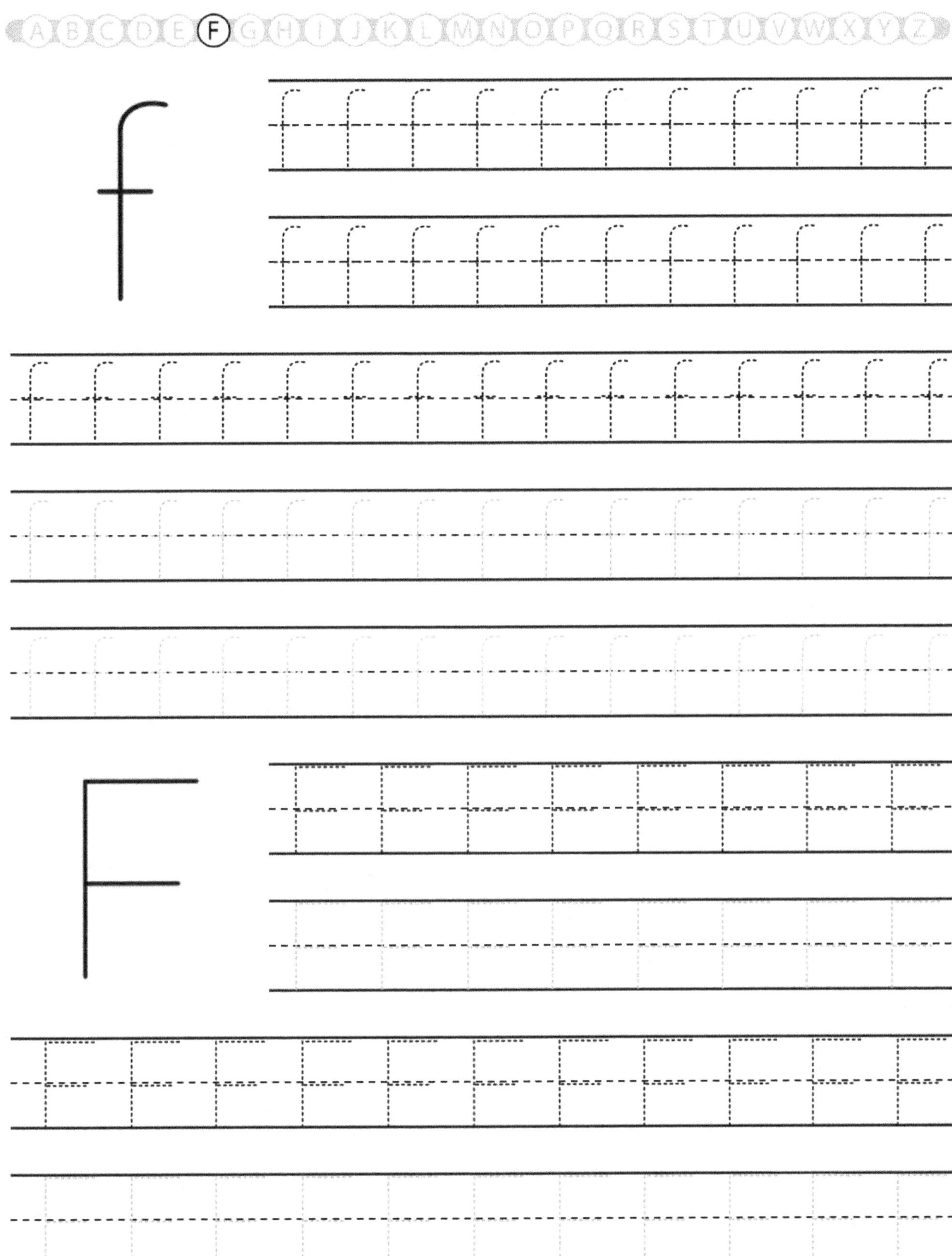

CONNECT THE DOTS

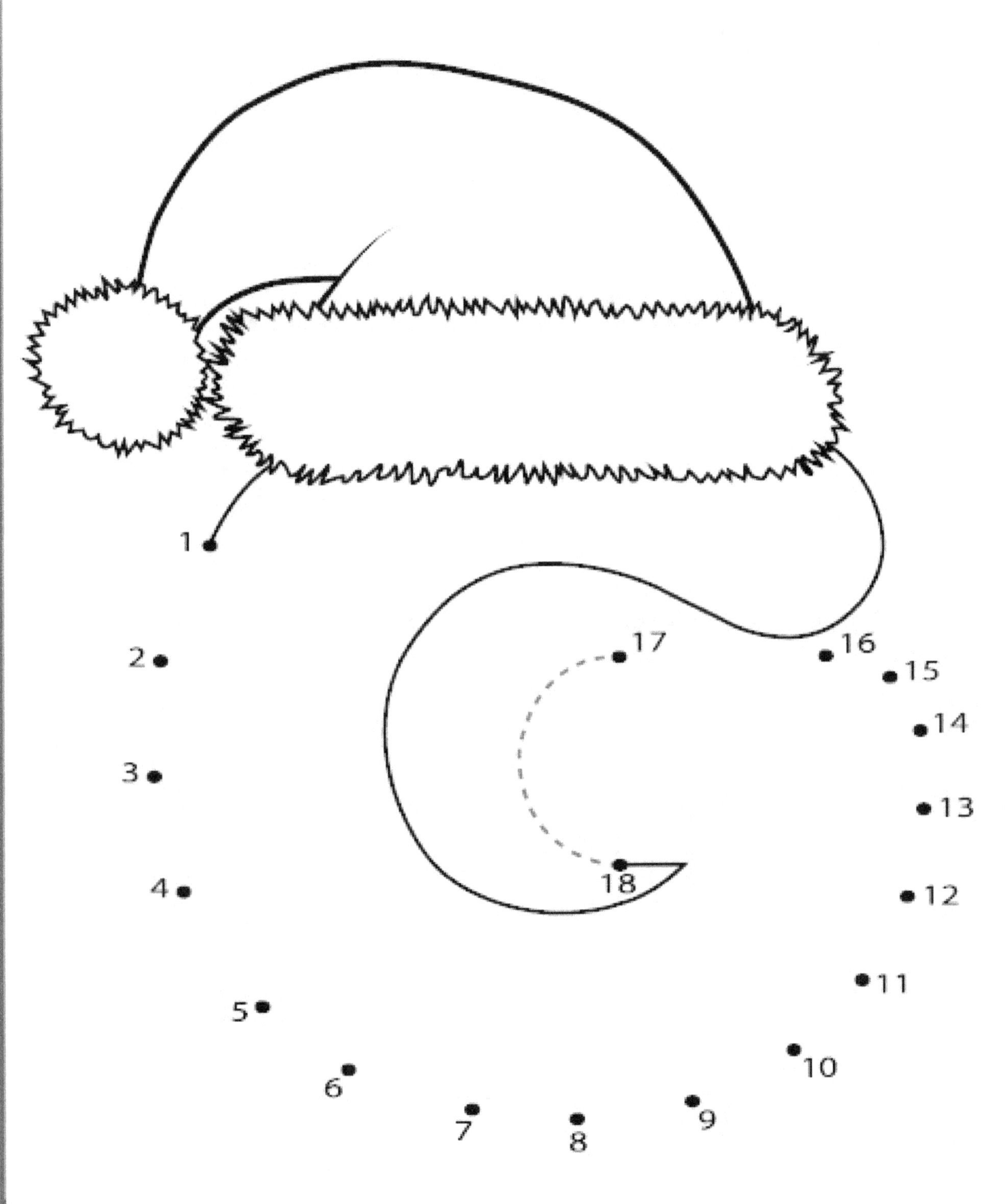

g

G

CONNECT THE DOTS

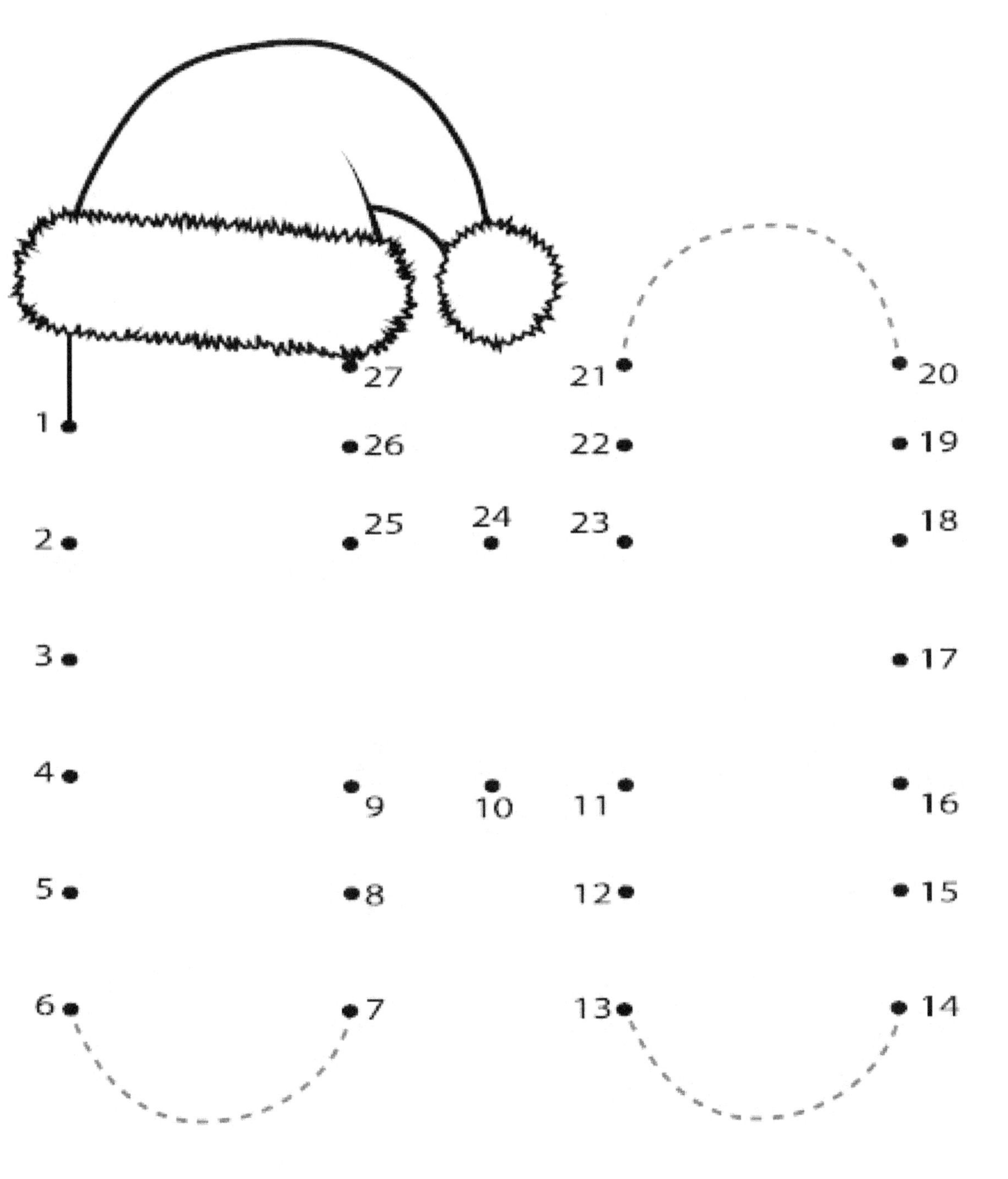

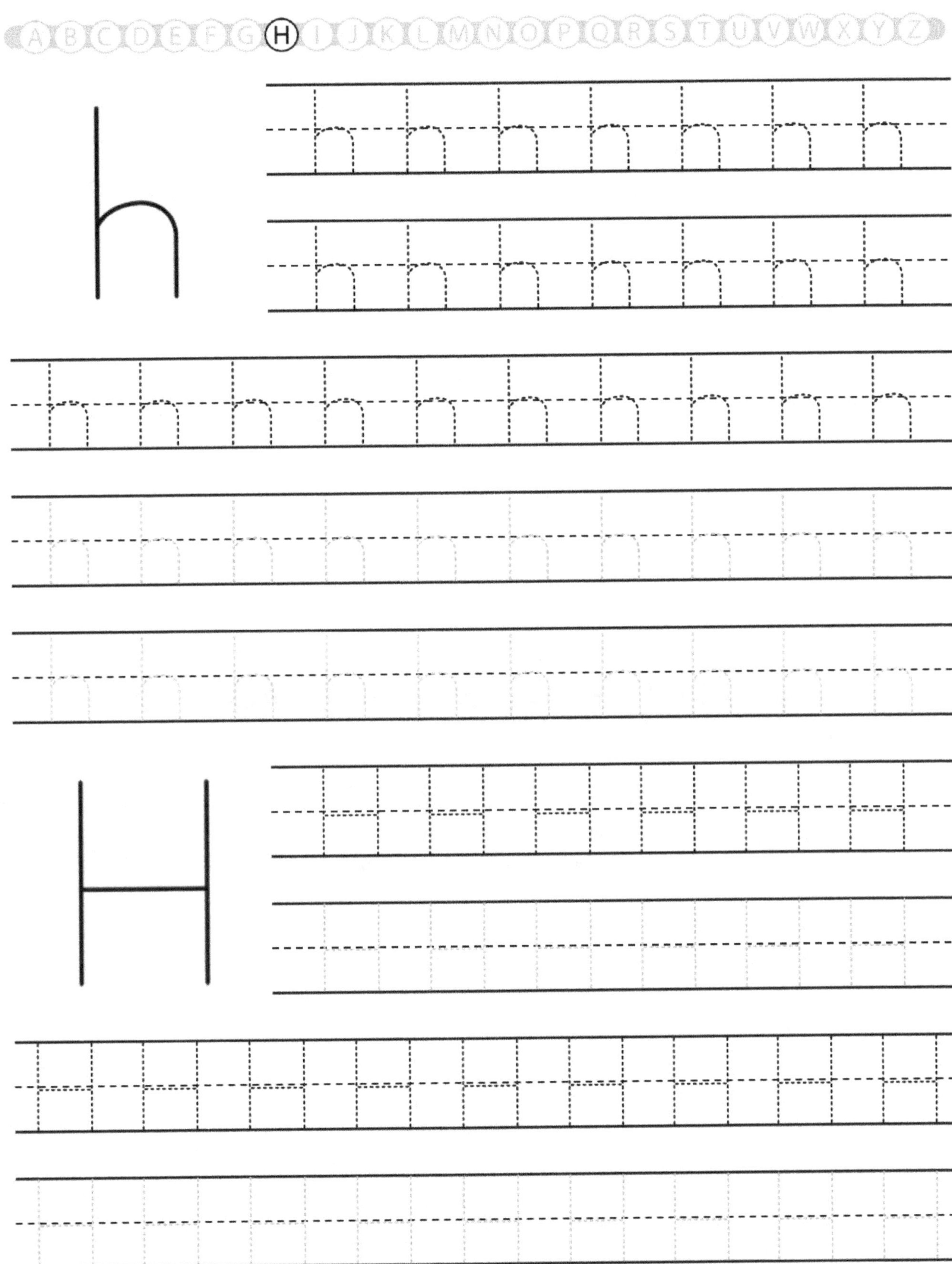

CONNECT THE DOTS

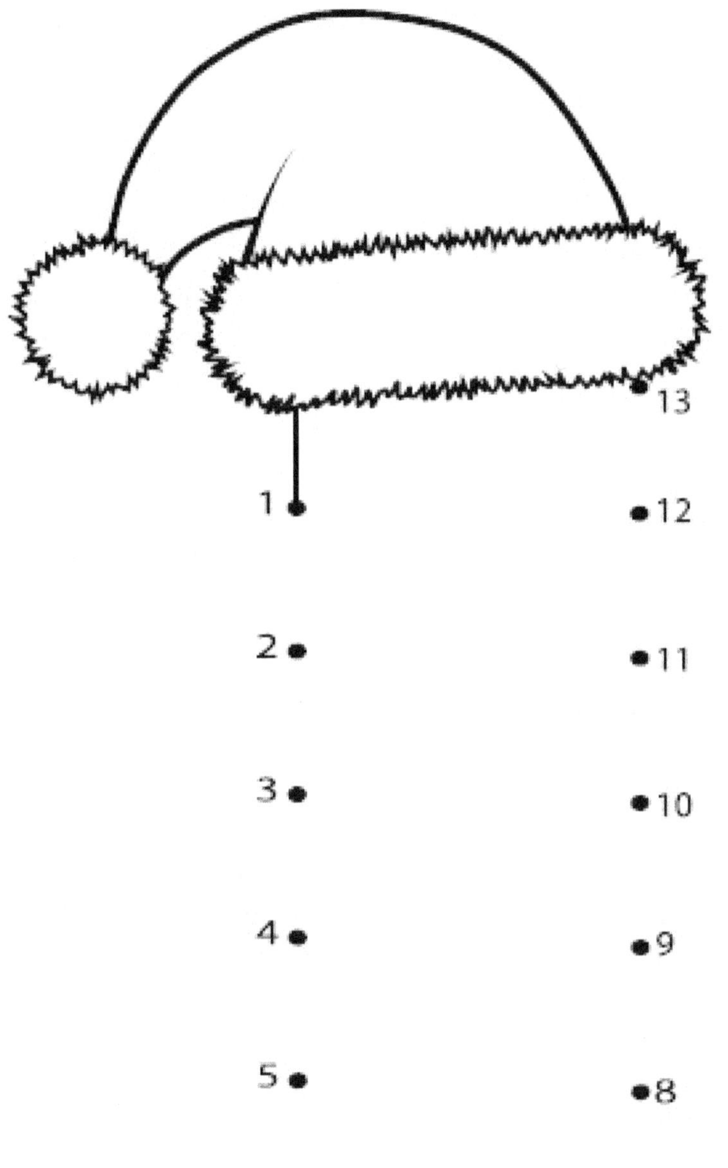

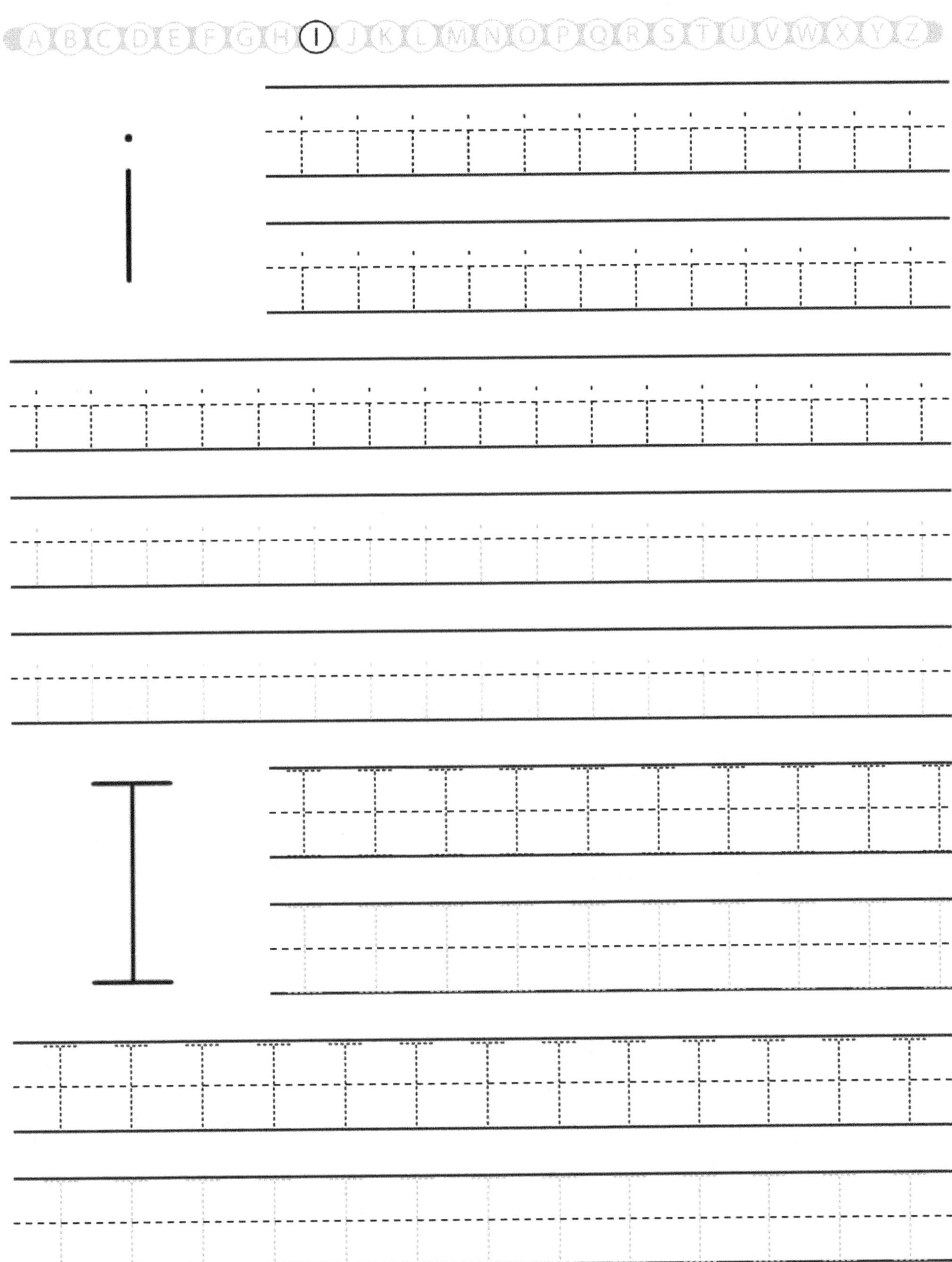

CONNECT THE DOTS

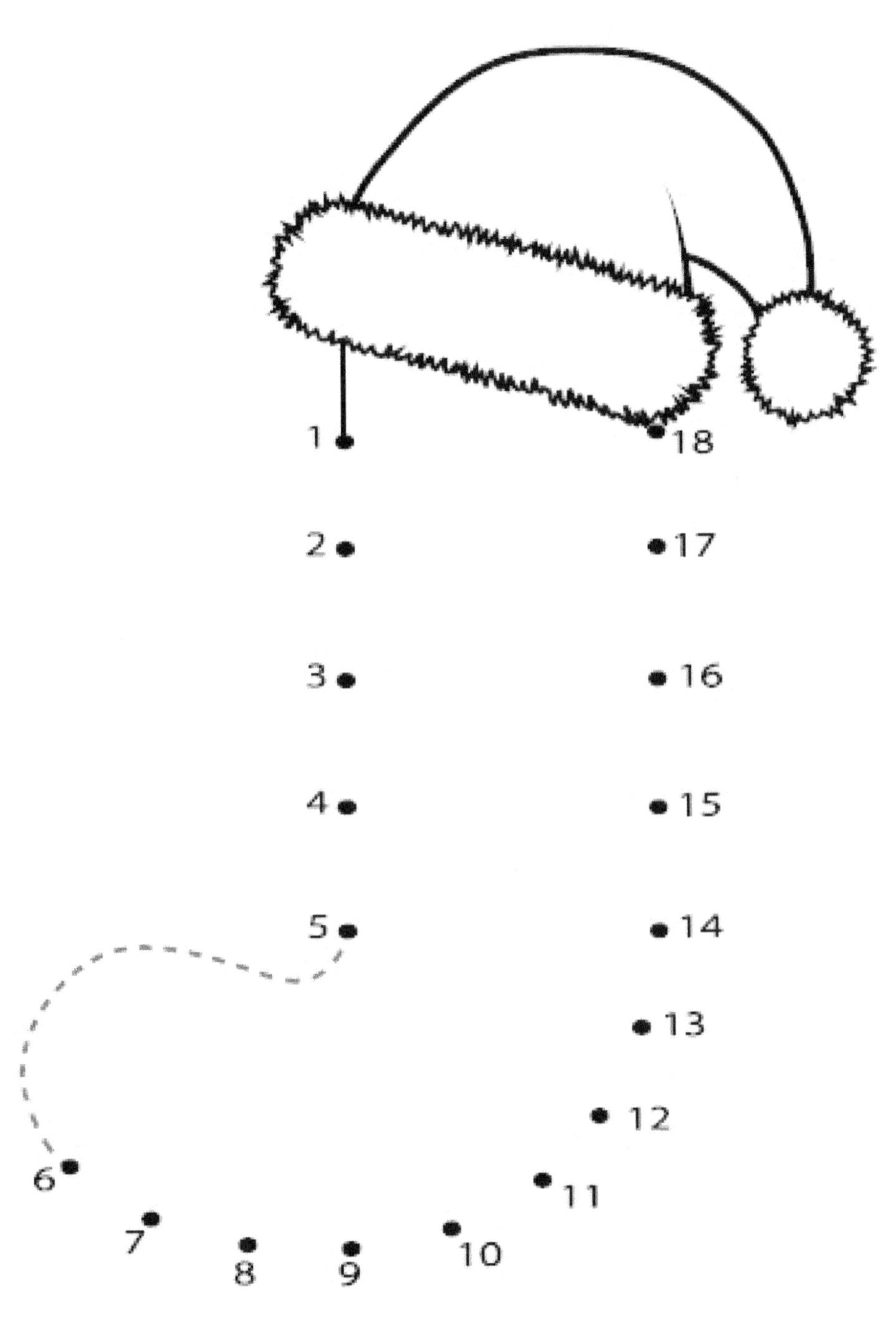

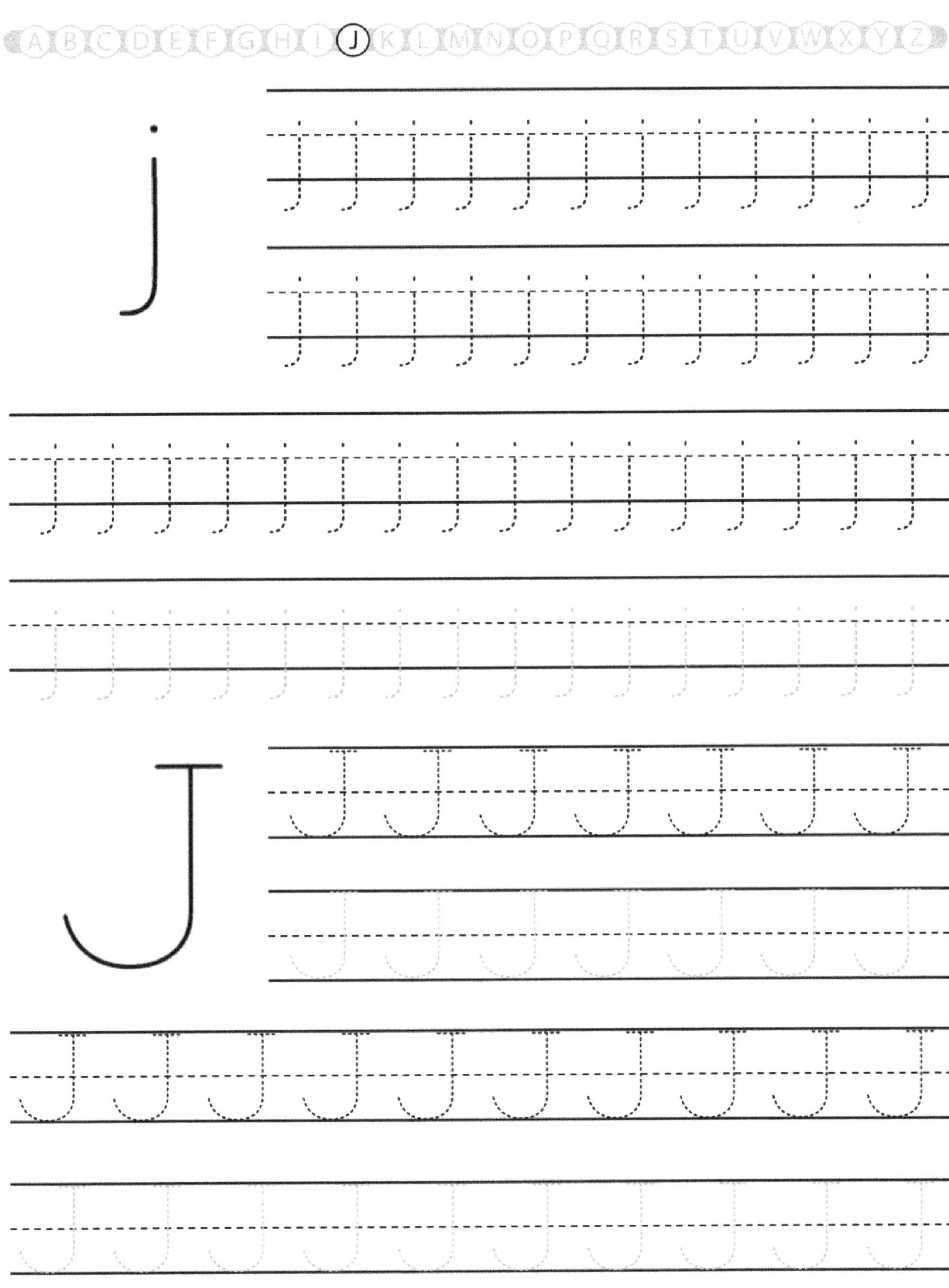

CONNECT THE DOTS

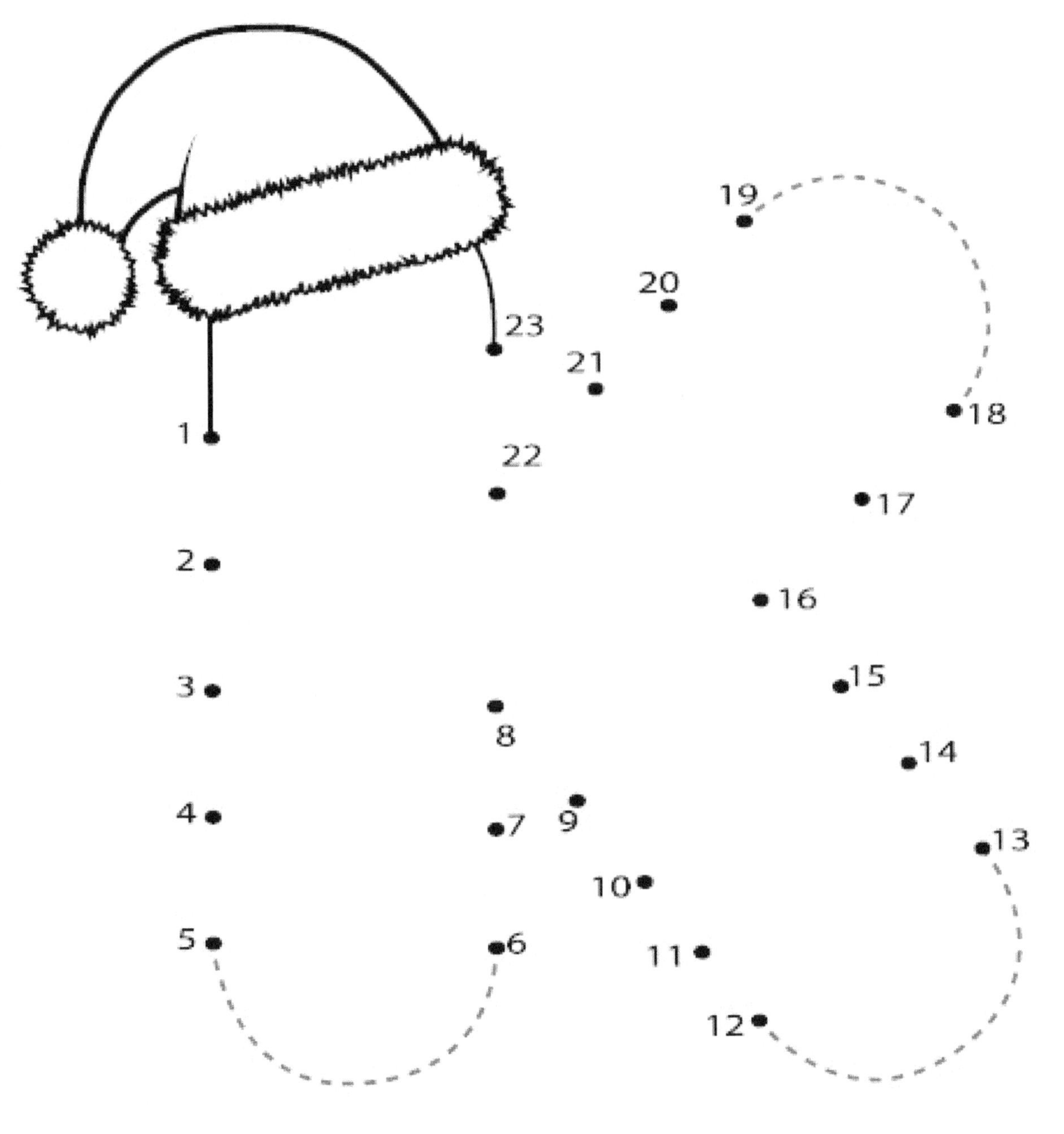

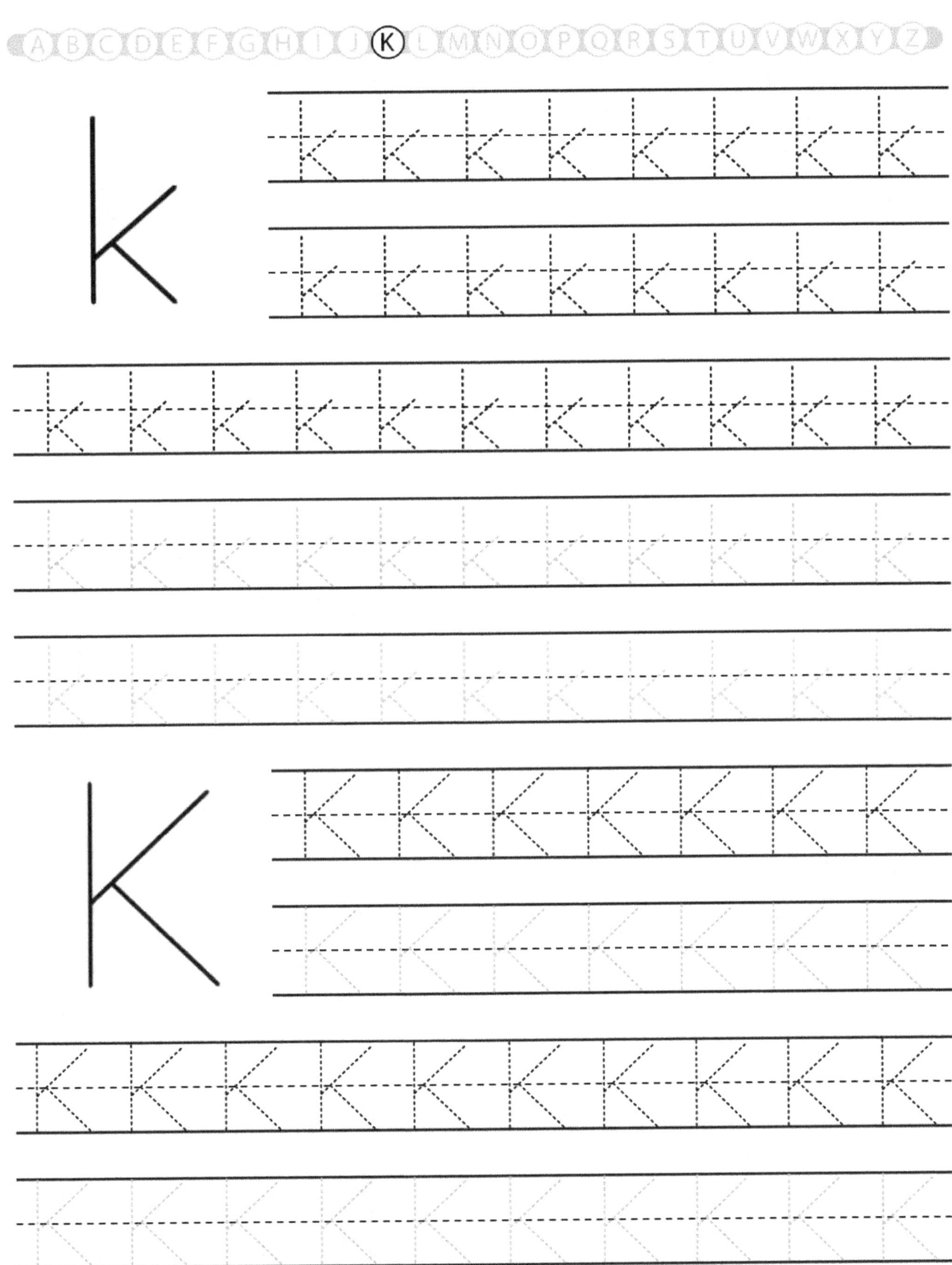

CONNECT THE DOTS

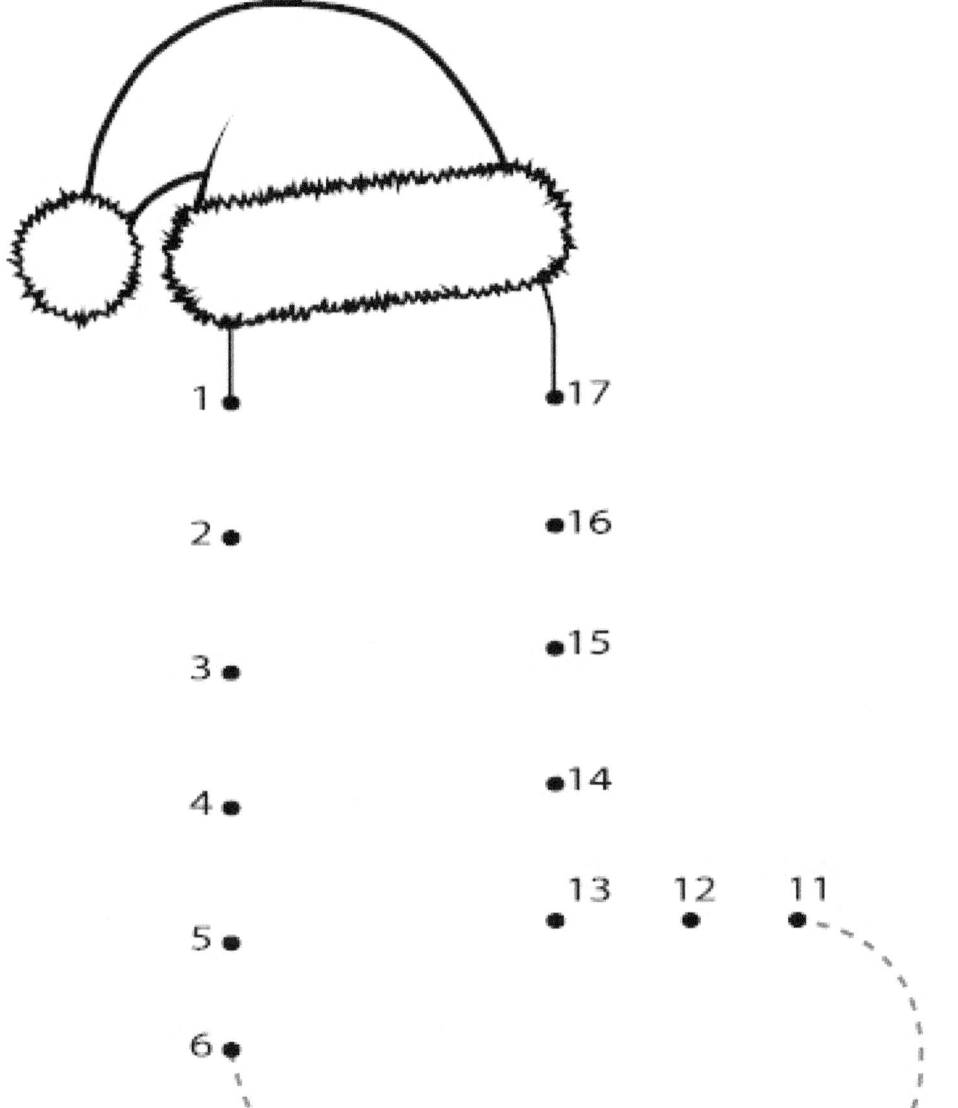

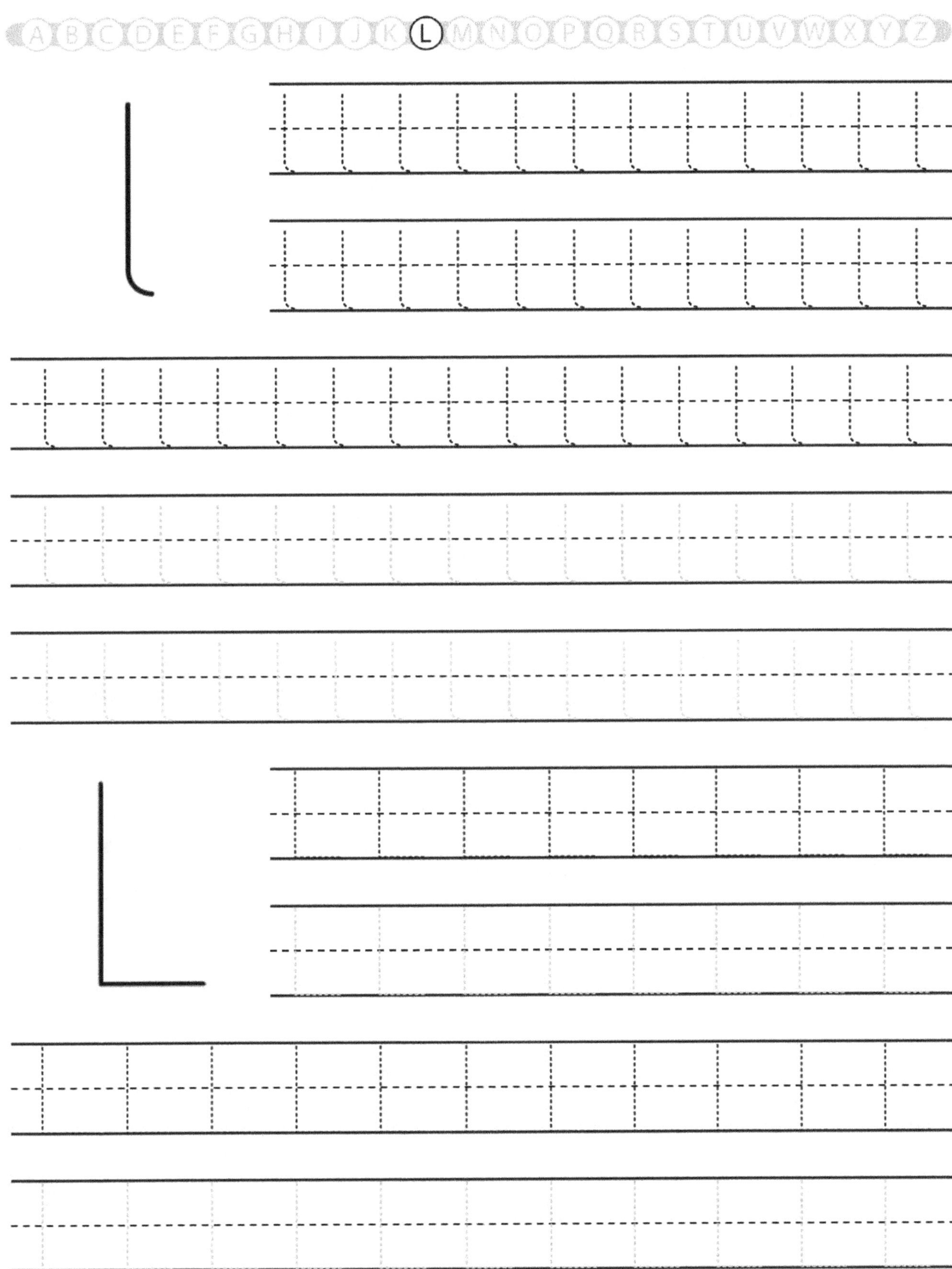

CONNECT THE DOTS

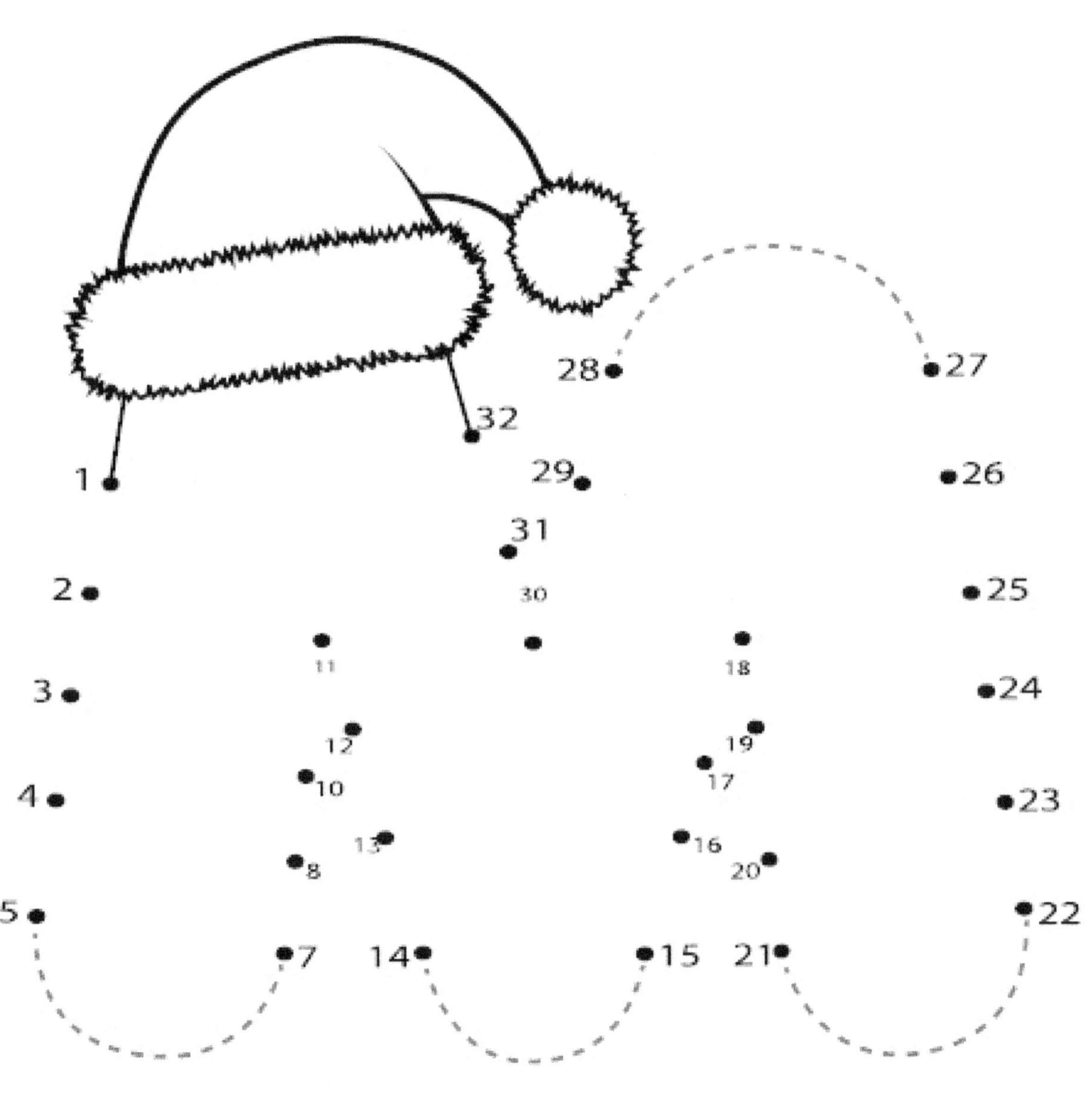

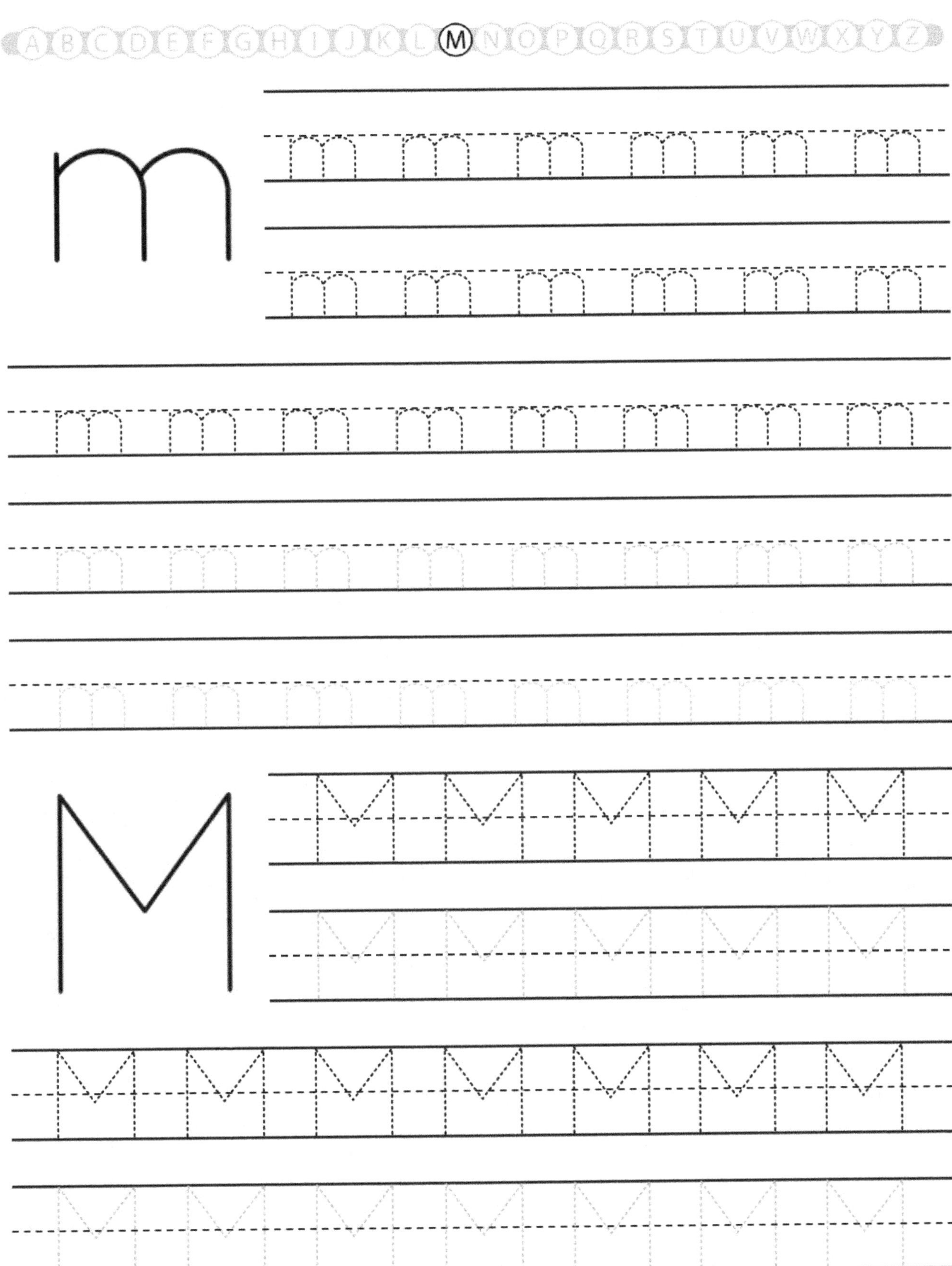

CONNECT THE DOTS

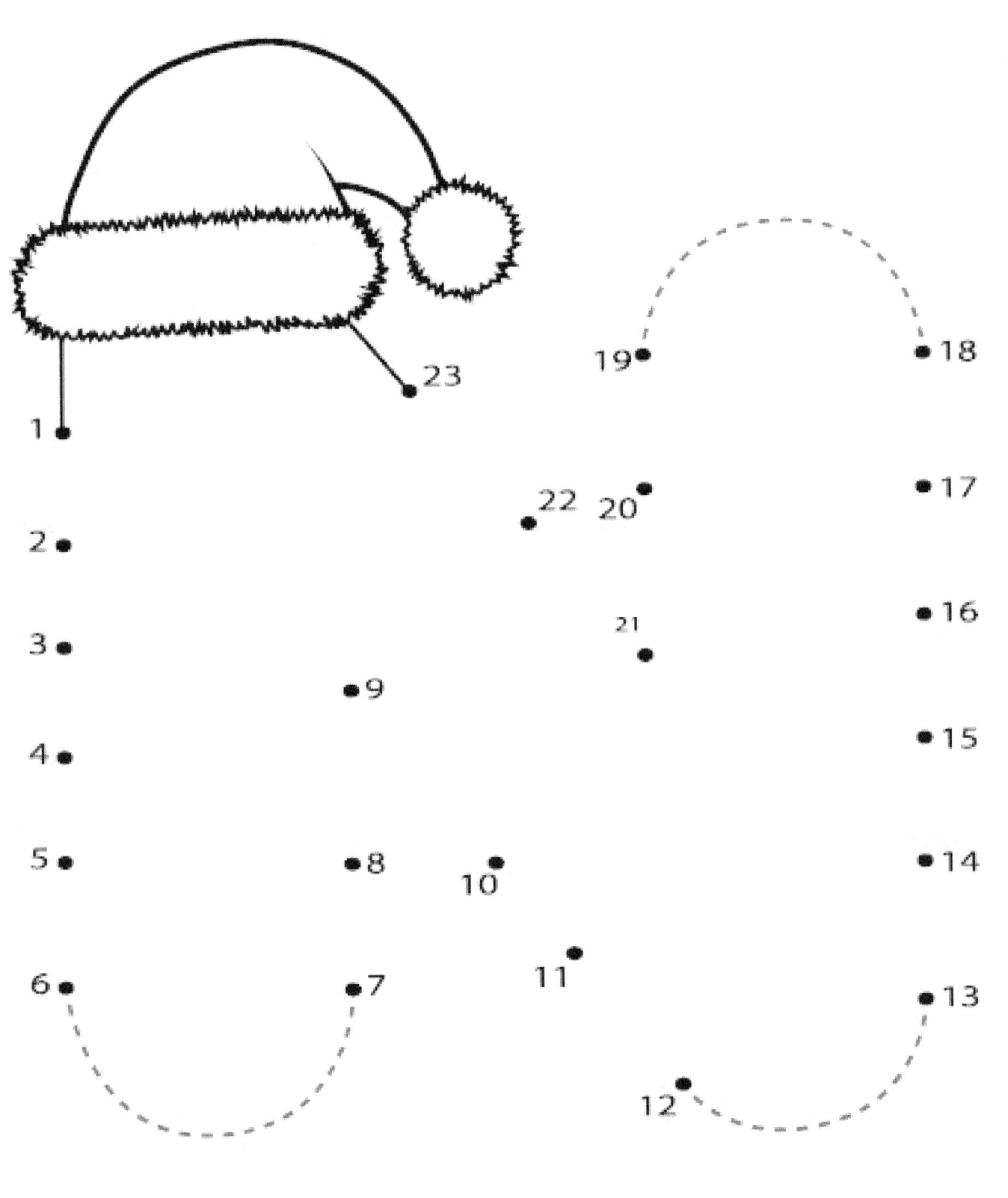

CONNECT THE DOTS

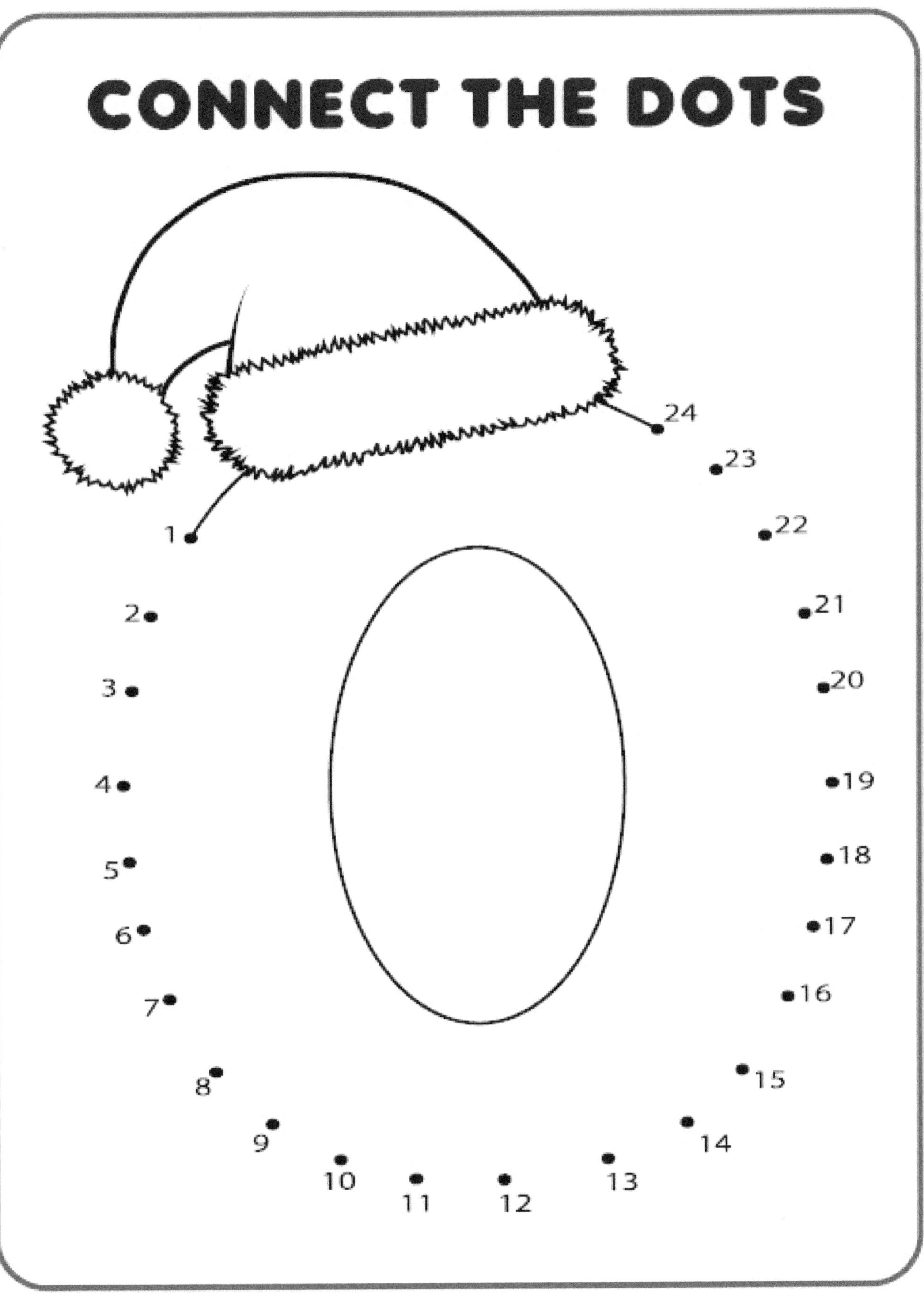

CONNECT THE DOTS

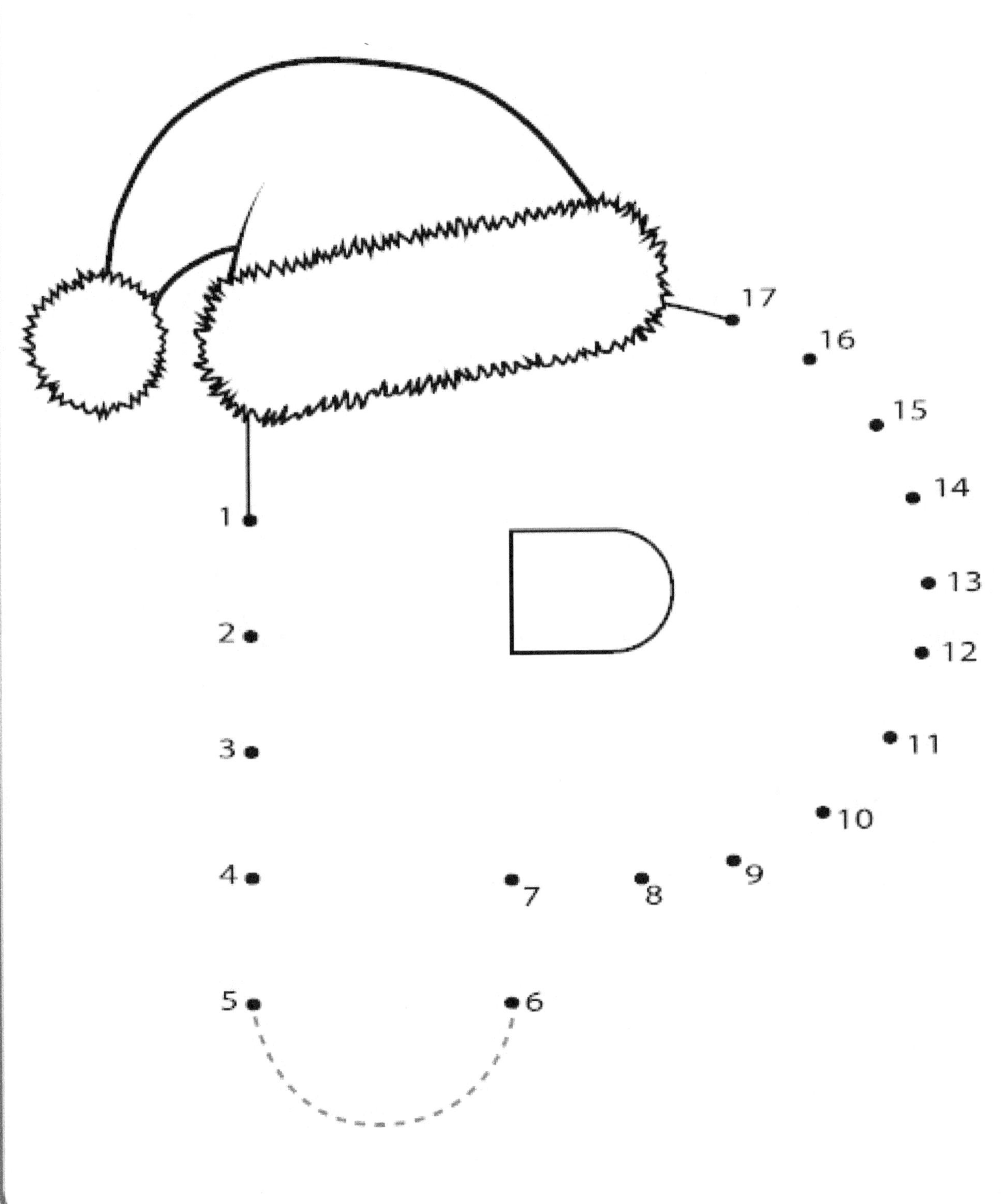

p

P

CONNECT THE DOTS

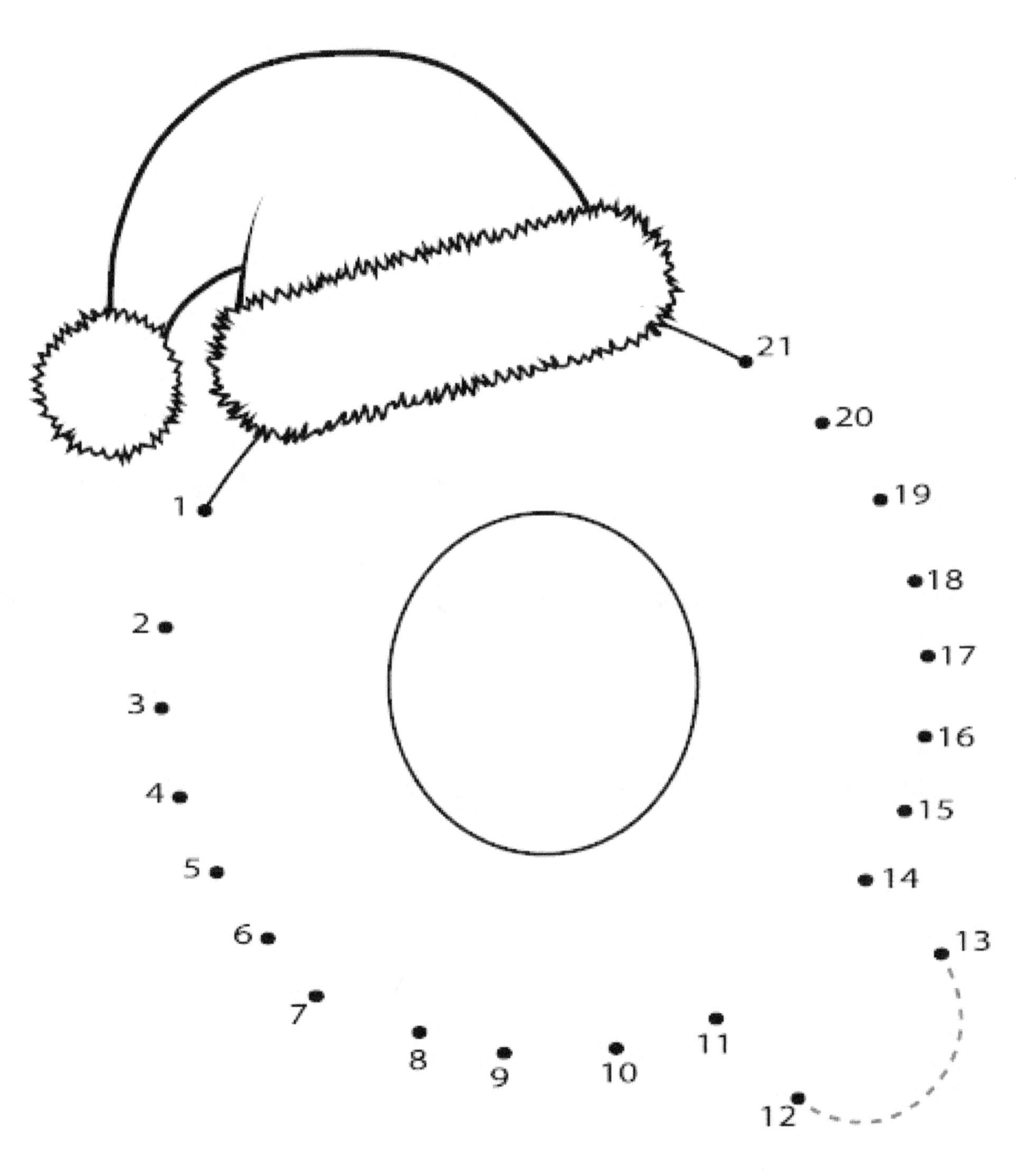

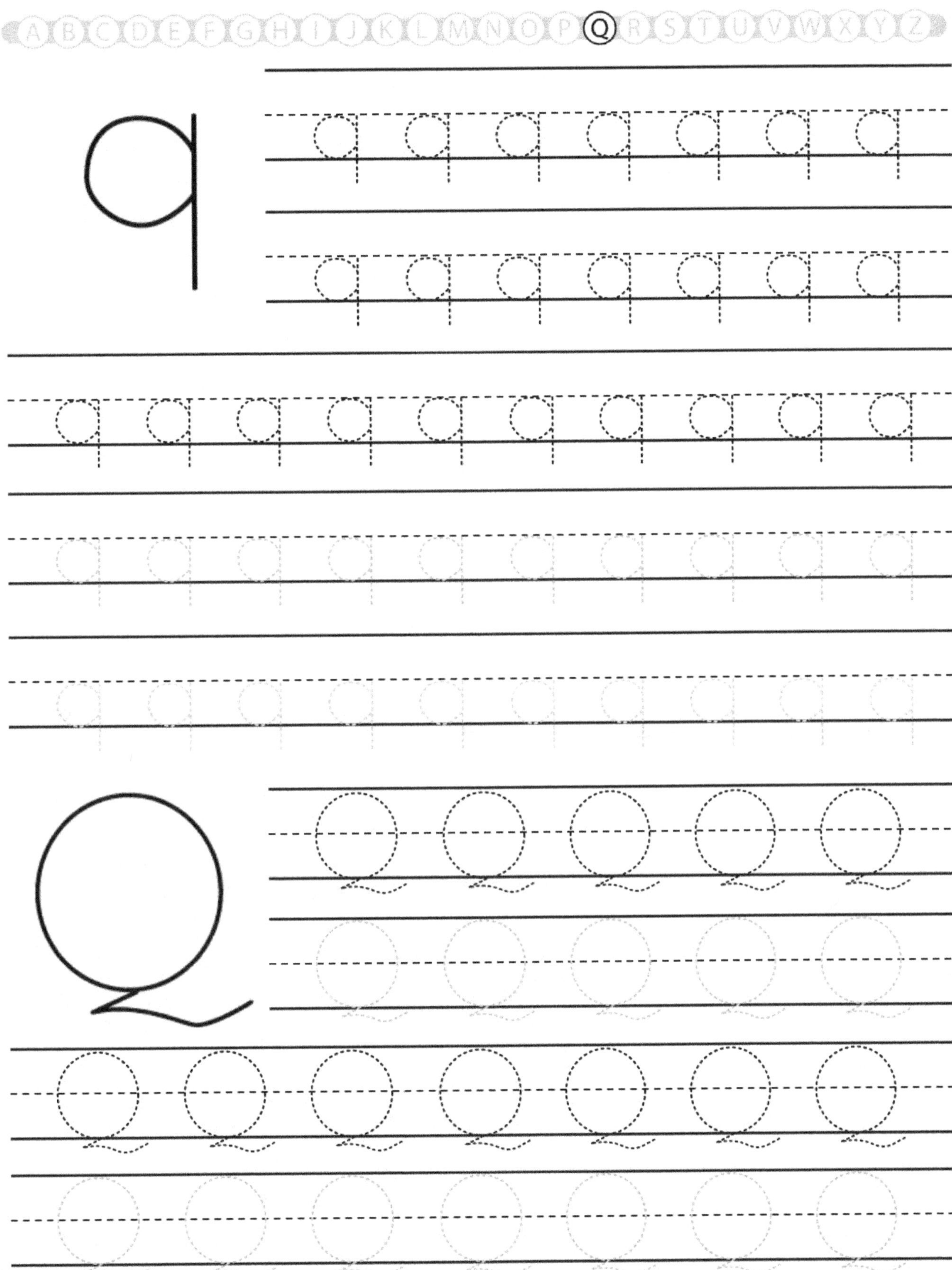

CONNECT THE DOTS

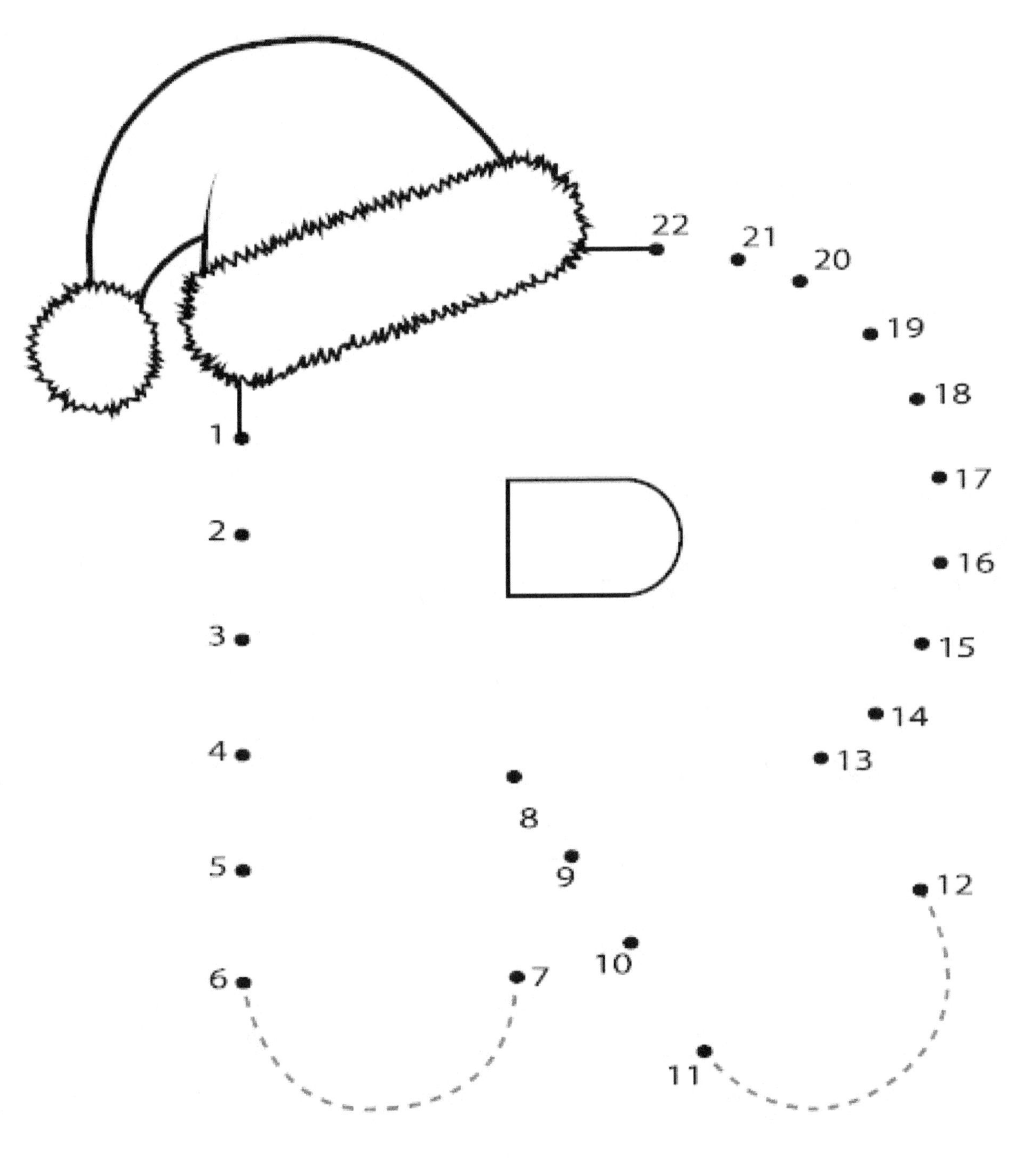

r

R

CONNECT THE DOTS

S

S

CONNECT THE DOTS

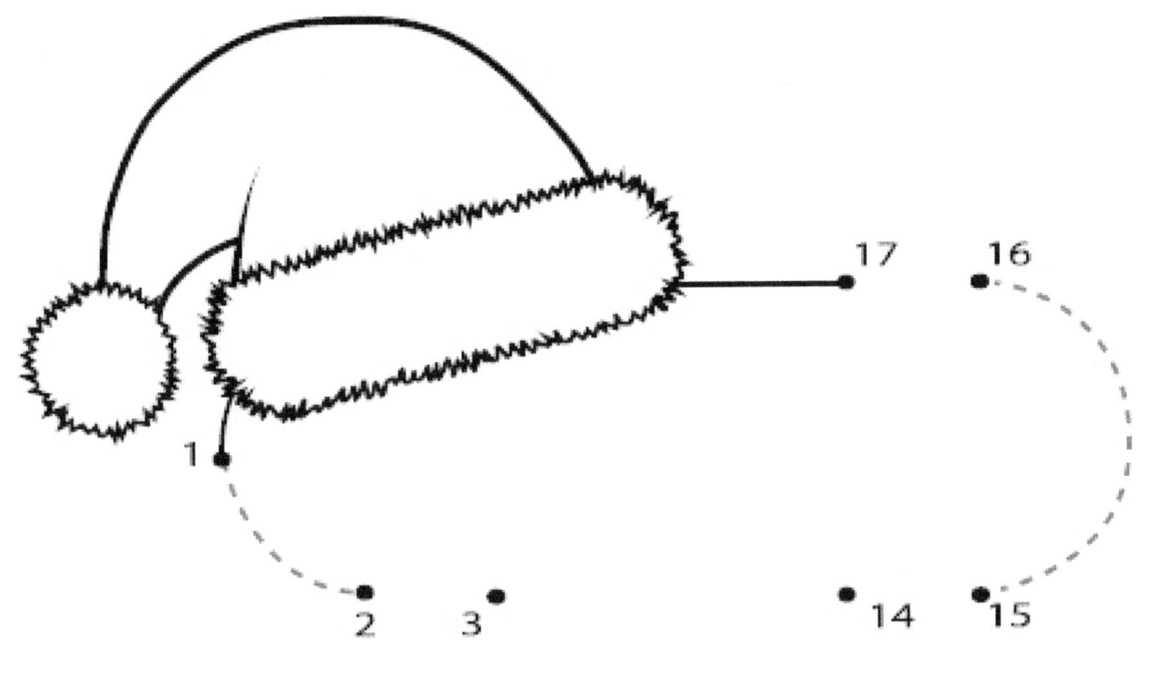

A B C D E F G H I J K L M N O P Q R S T U V W X Y Z

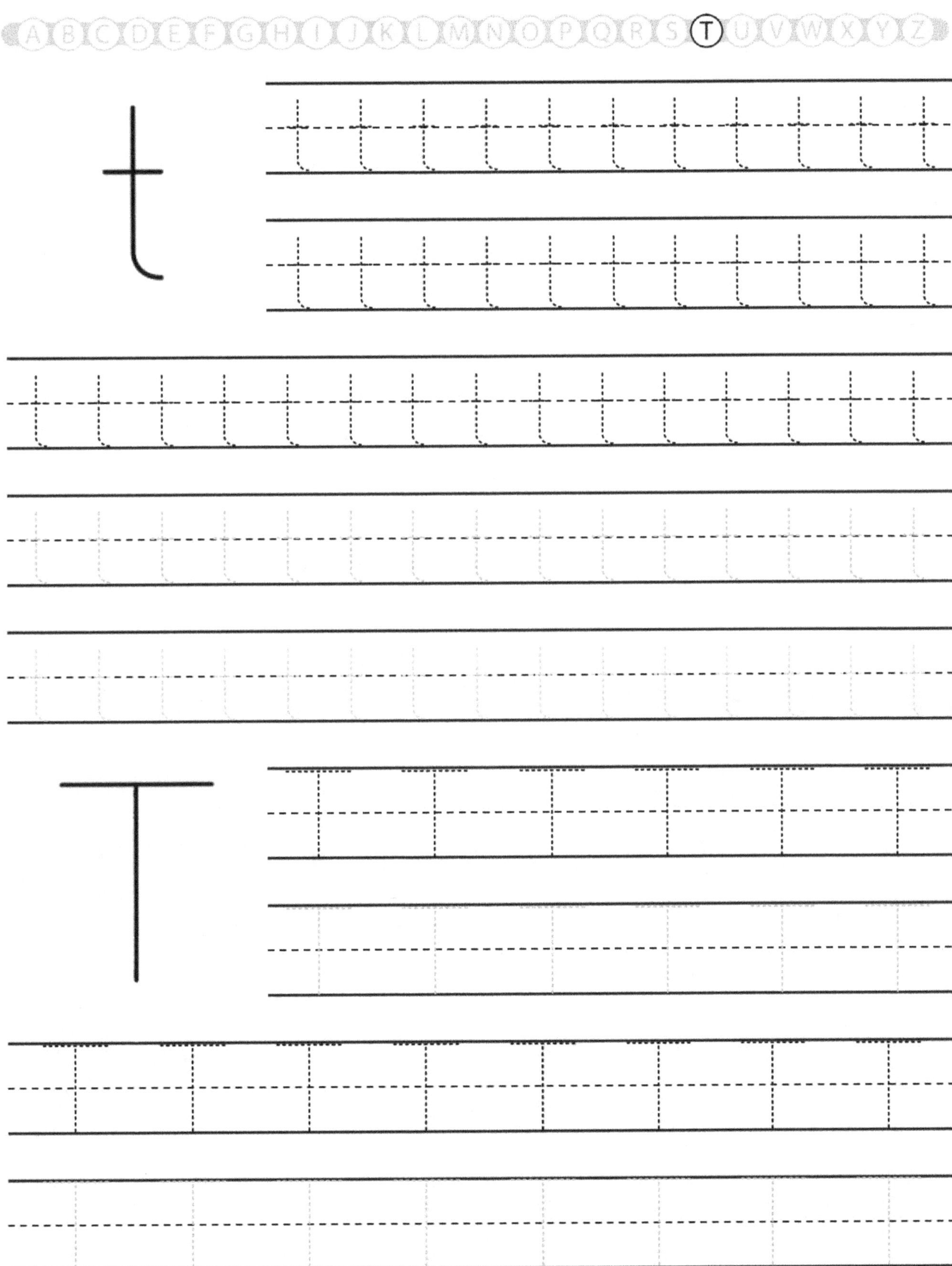

CONNECT THE DOTS

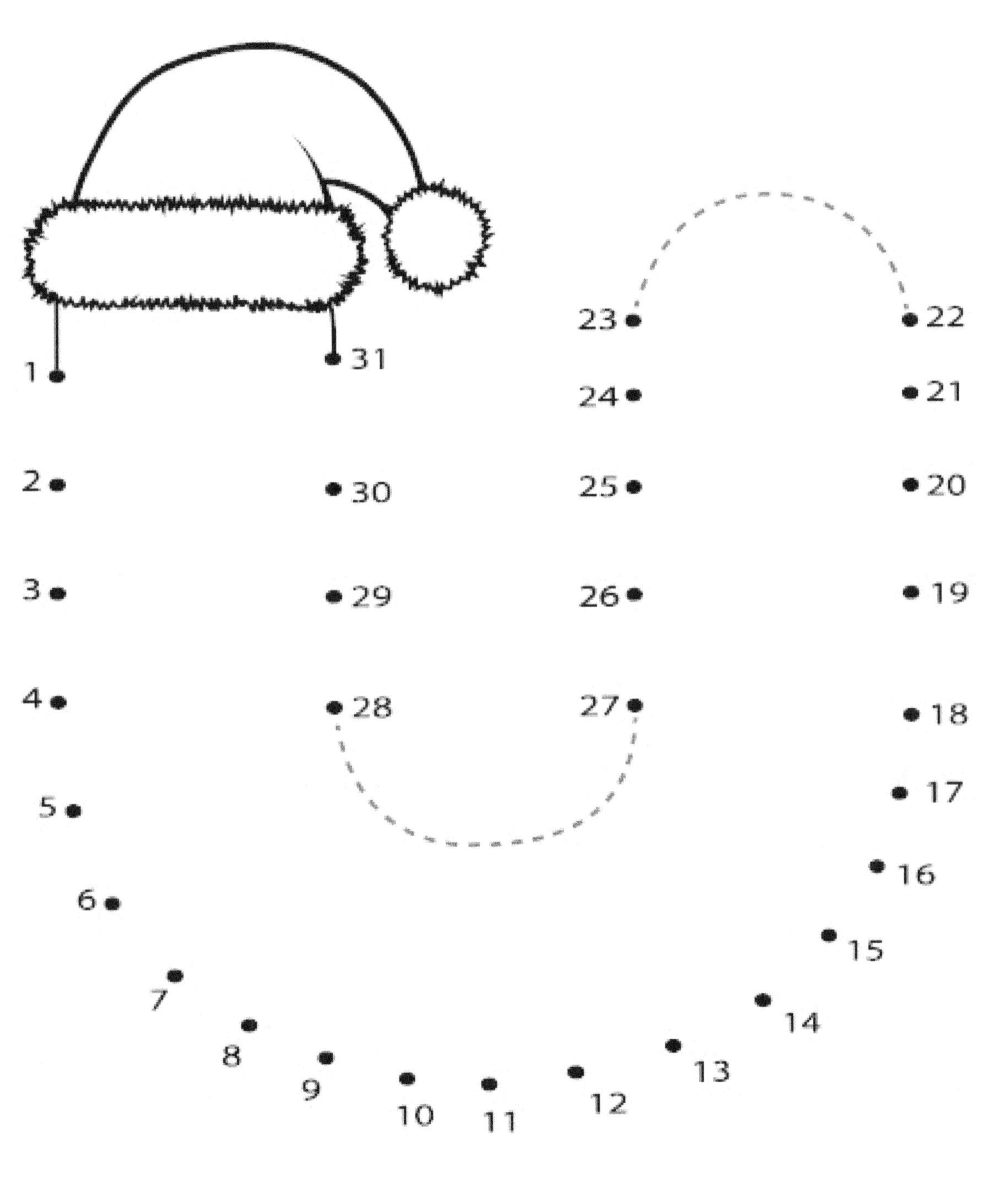

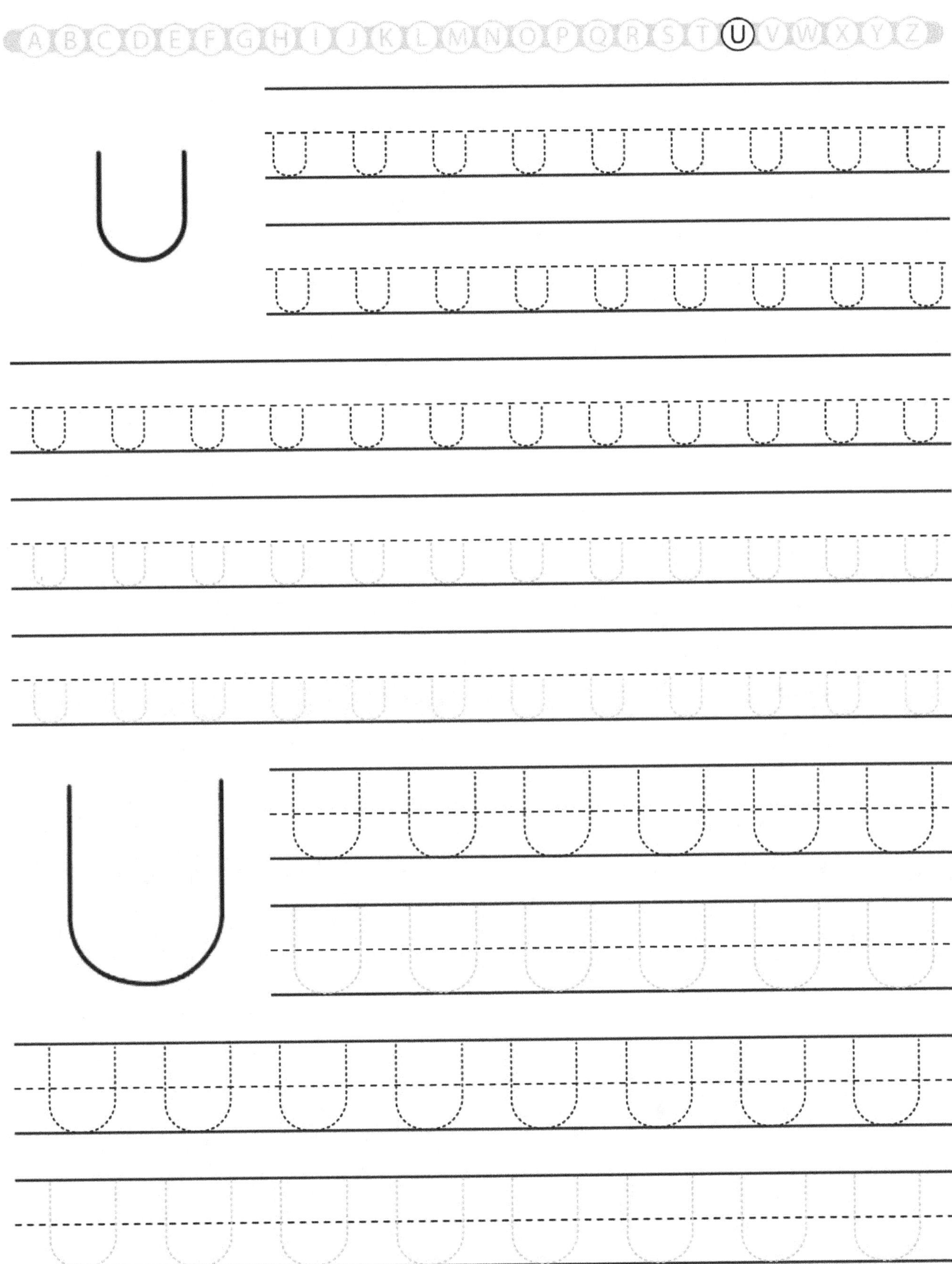

CONNECT THE DOTS

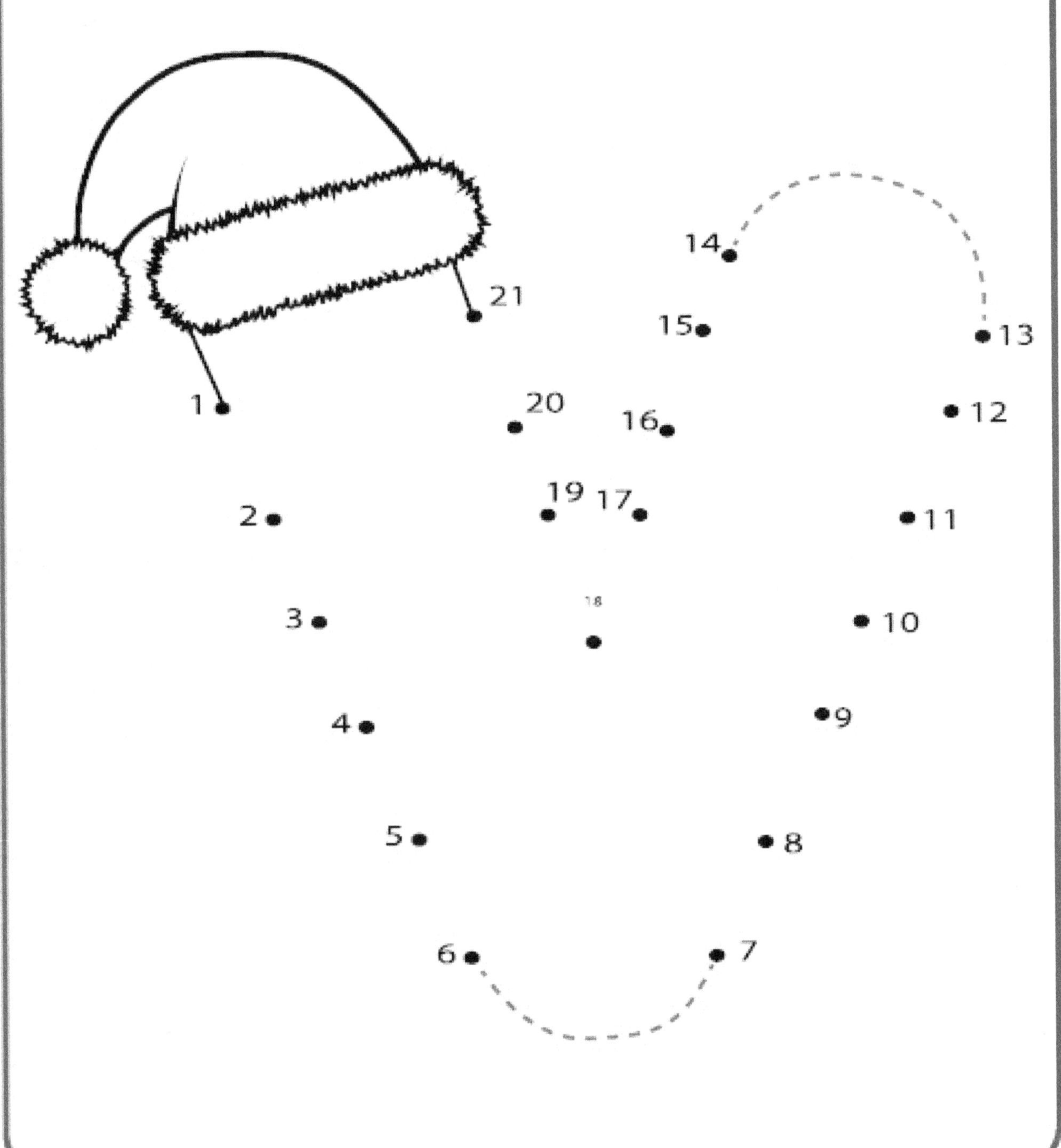

CONNECT THE DOTS

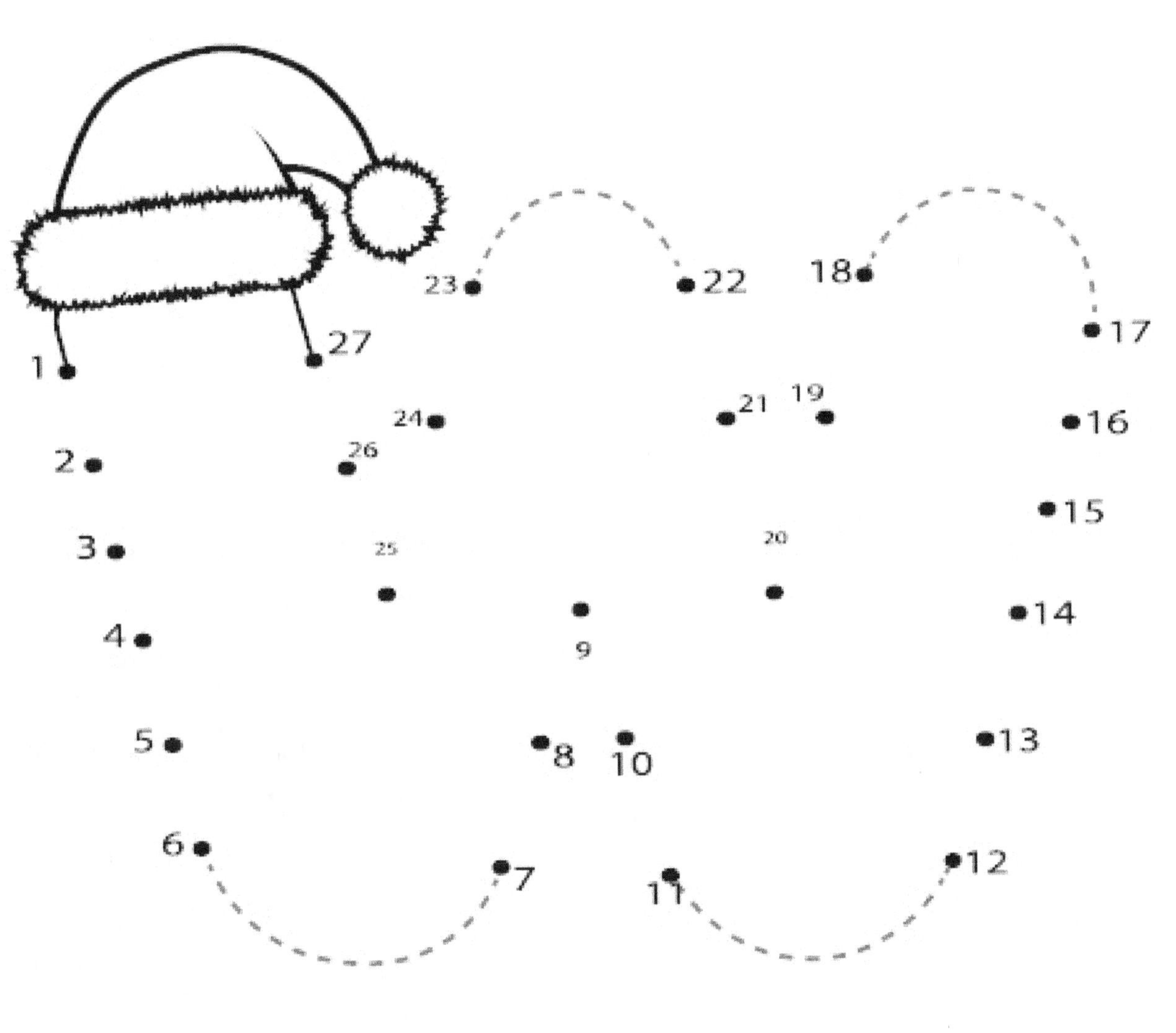

CONNECT THE DOTS

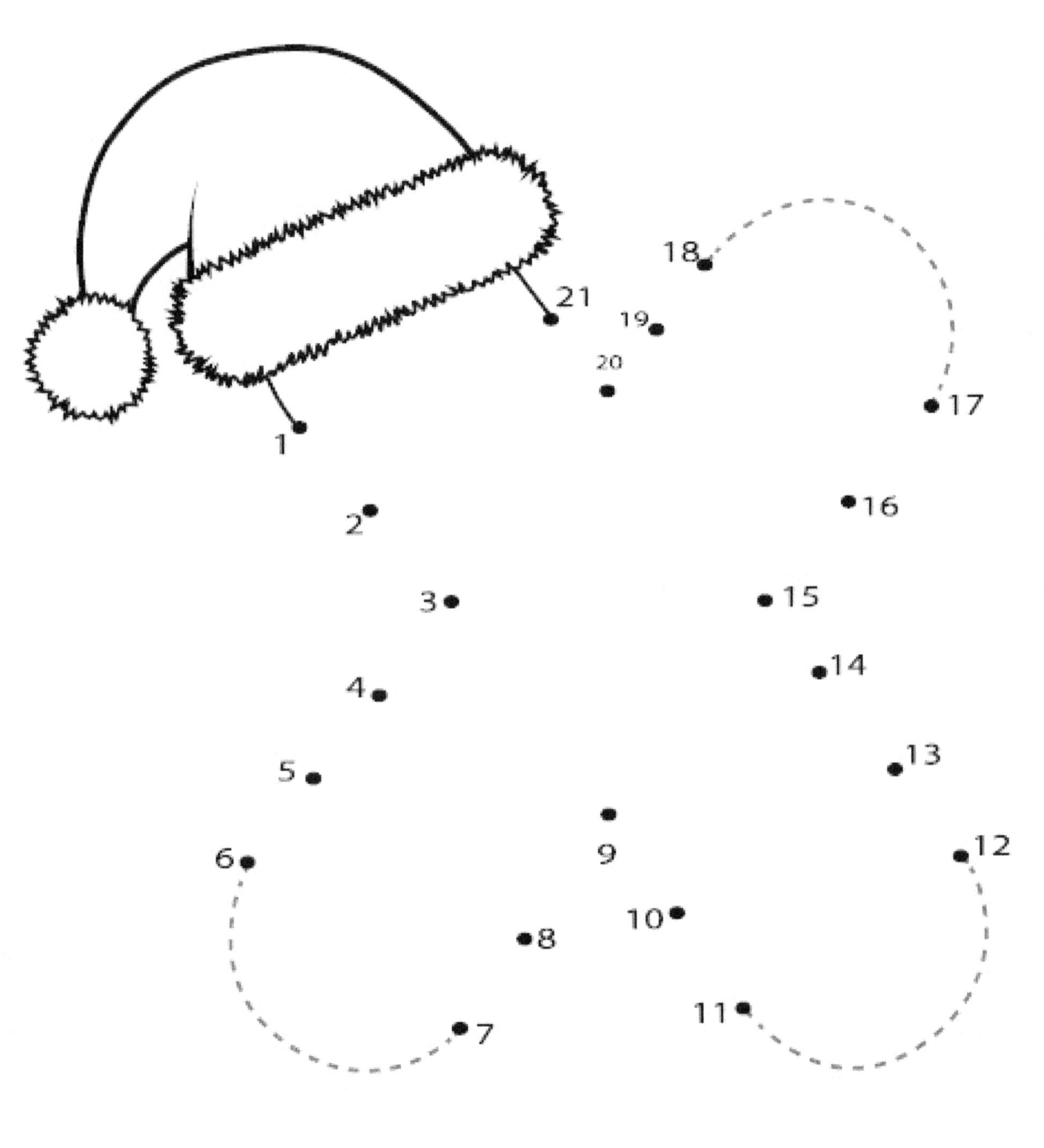

CONNECT THE DOTS

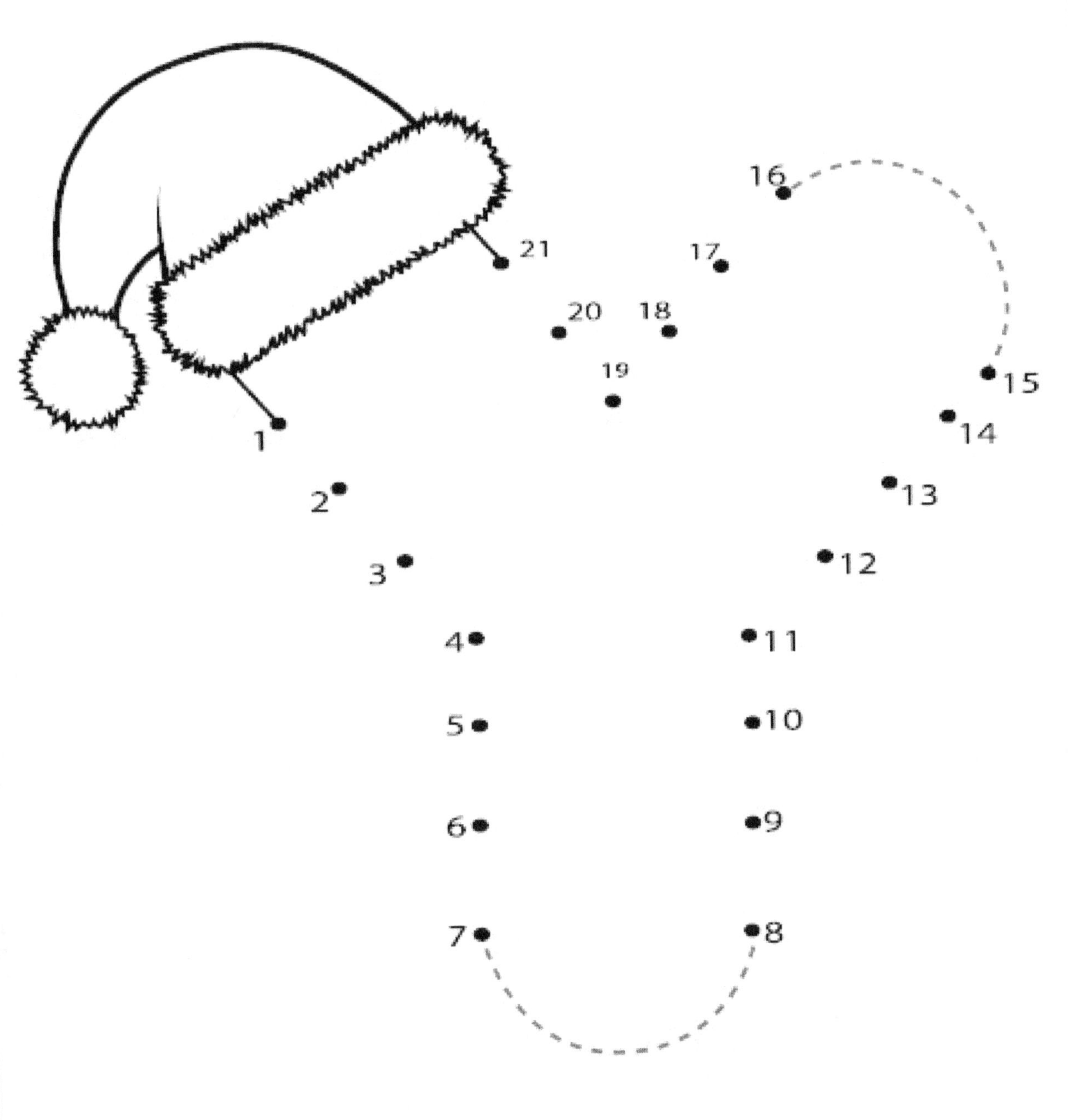

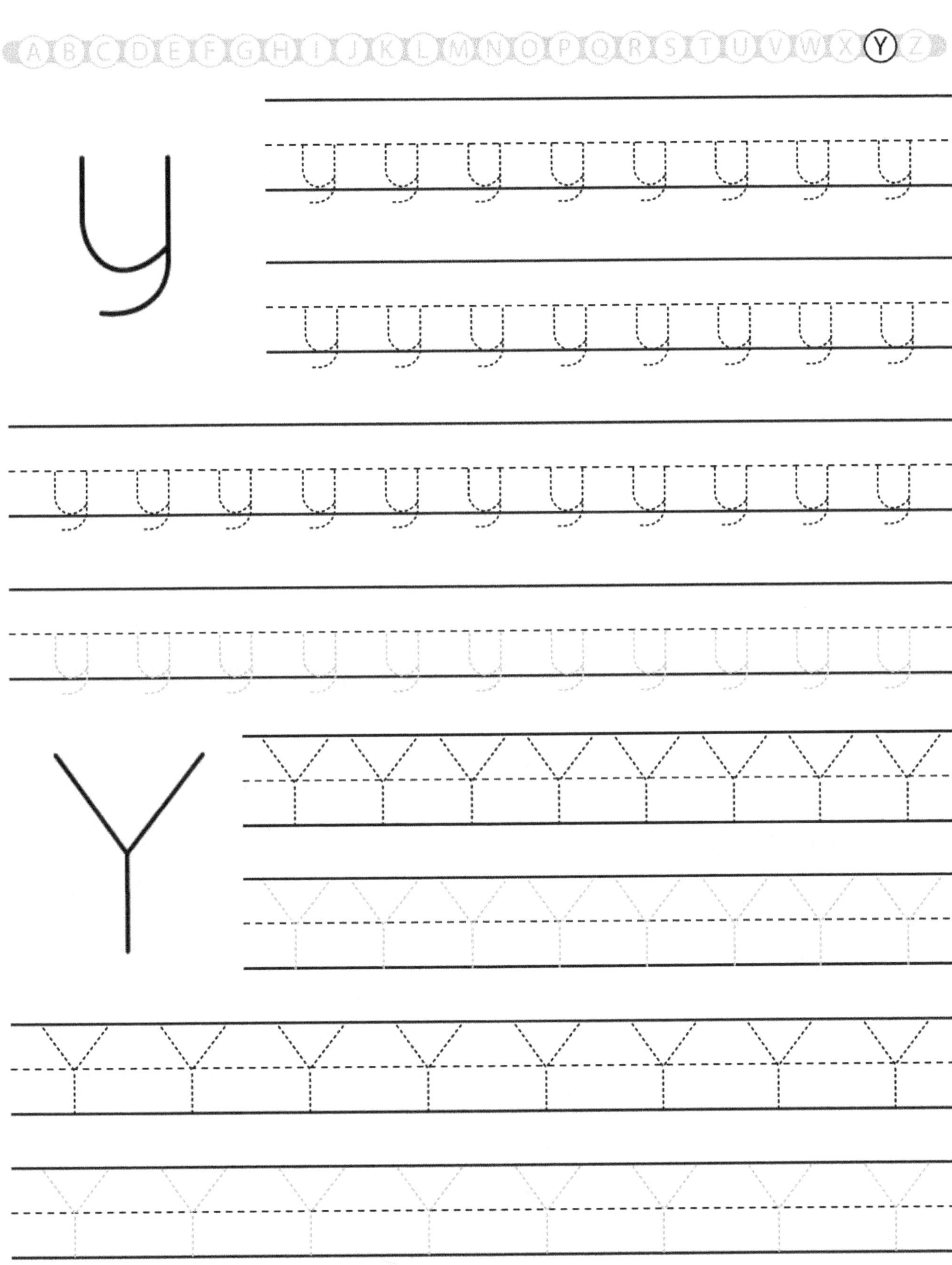

CONNECT THE DOTS

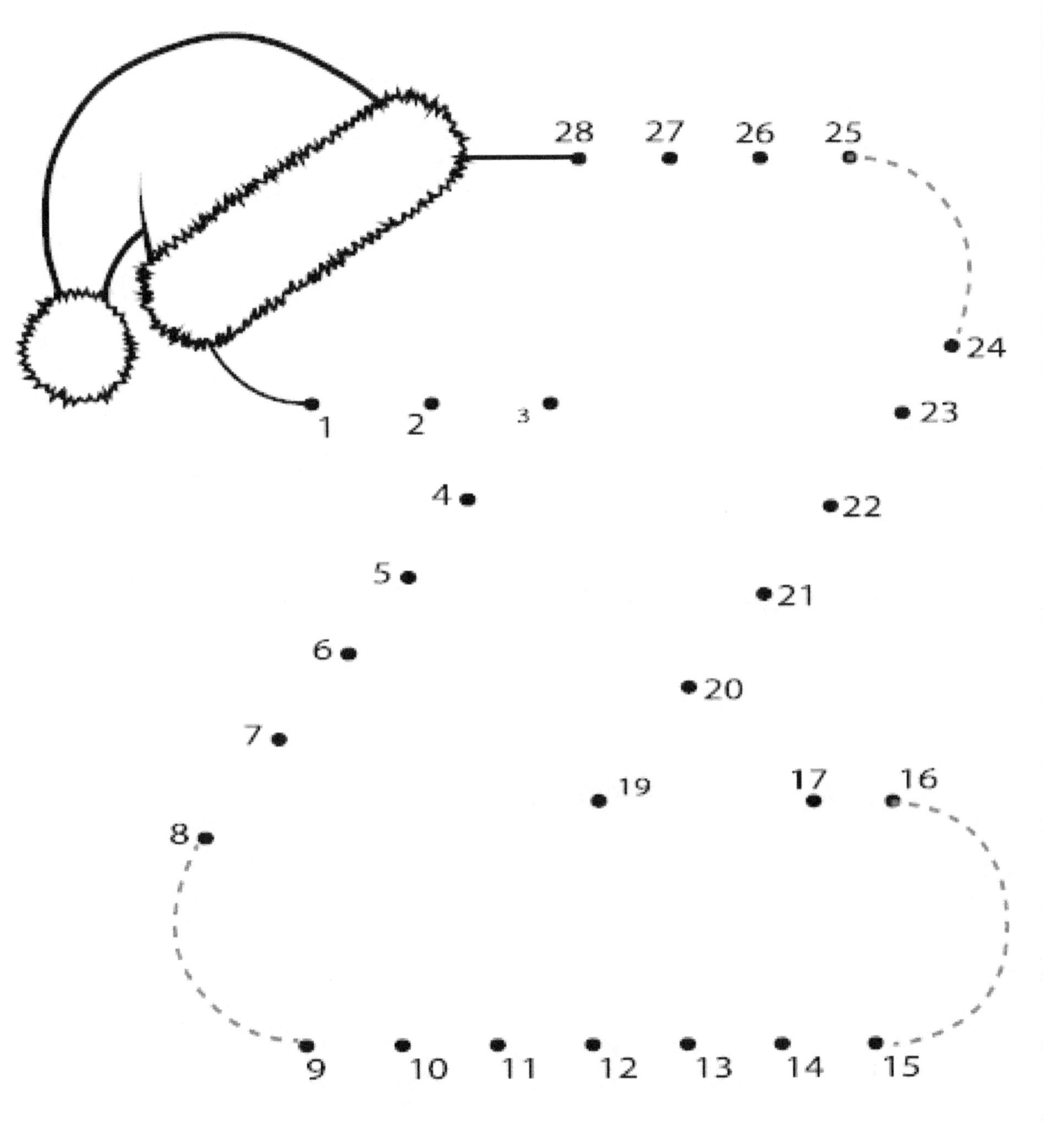

Z

z

FINISH THE ALPHABET

ALPHABET WORKSHEET

Cut out the letter and paste them in
the correct spots

A		C	D		F
	H	I			L
M		O	P	Q	
S		U	V		X
	Z				

B	E	G	J	K
N	R	T	W	Y

MAZES

TIK TAK TOE